INDIA AND HER PEOPLE

INDIA AND HER PEOPLE

By

Swami Abhedananda

GYAN

Published by

Gyan Publishing House
5, Ansari Road
Darayaganj, New Delhi-110002
Phone: 011-47034999, 9811692060
E-mail: books@gyanbooks.com

Distribution Network
gyanbooks.com
India, USA, Canada, UK, Australia

ISBN: 978-93-6208-236-7 (HB)
First Published, 1906

2nd Impression 2024

Printed at: Gyan Press, Delhi.

INDIA AND HER PEOPLE
Author: SWAMI ABHEDANANDA

SWAMI ABHEDANANDA

INDIA

AND

HER PEOPLE

BY

SWAMI ABHEDANANDA

Author of "Self-Knowledge," "How to be a Yogi," "Spiritual Unfoldment," "Divine Heritage of Man," "Philosophy of Work" etc.

THIRD EDITION

PUBLISHED BY

THE VEDANTA SOCIETY

NEW YORK

TO THE

PEOPLE OF INDIA

WITH DEEP FELLOW-FEELING

AND

EARNEST PRAYERS FOR THE RESTORATION

OF THEIR ANCIENT GLORY

AND

NATIONAL FREEDOM

INTRODUCTION.

I AM very glad to learn that the course of lectures, recently delivered before the Brooklyn Institute of Arts and Sciences by Swami Abhedananda, is to be published. These lectures constitute an exceedingly valuable description of the social, political, educational, and religious conditions of India. They contain precisely what the American wants to know about India. Delivered, as they were, by a native of India, they are not colored by foreign prejudices. I am impressed, by what I heard of the lectures, with the fact that in the hurry and bustle of our Western civilization we have a great deal to learn from the East.

FRANKLIN W. HOOPER,

Director of the Brooklyn Institute of Arts and Sciences.

BROOKLYN, N. Y., April 26, 1906.

PREFACE.

THE first six lectures contained in this volume were delivered before the Brooklyn Institute of Arts and Sciences. As my limited time did not permit me to describe at length the status of Hindu women, I have added a separate lecture on "Woman's Place in Hindu Religion" to complete the subject.

My main object has been to give an impartial account of the facts from the standpoint of an unbiased historian, and to remove all misunderstandings which prevail among the Americans concerning India and her people. I have cited Hindu, American, and European authorities to support my statements, and I beg to acknowledge my indebtedness to those writers from whom I have quoted, especially to Mr. R. C. Dutt, C.I.E., for numerous valuable facts and statistics collected by him through years of tireless research in England, and embodied in his historical works, "Civilization in Ancient India," "Economic History of India," and "India in the Victorian Age."

THE AUTHOR.

NEW YORK, May 15, 1906.

CONTENTS.

INDIA AND HER PEOPLE.

I.

THE PREVAILING PHILOSOPHY OF TO-DAY.

CENTURIES before the Christian era, nay, long before the advent of the prophet and founder of Judaism, when the forefathers of the Anglo-Saxon races were living in caves and forests, tattooing their bodies, eating raw animal flesh, wearing animal skins,—in that remote antiquity, the dawn of true civilization broke upon the horizon of India, or *Bhârata Varsha*, as it is called in Sanskrit.

The ancient Vedic sages had already perfected their lofty system of moral philosophy, and their followers were well-established in the practice of the ethical and spiritual teachings of the

Vedas even before Moses* had reformed the lawless and nomadic tribes of Israel by giving them the ten commandments in the name of Jahveh. And while thinkers among the Semitic tribes were still trying to explain the origin of the human race and of the universe through the mythological stories of creation collected from the Chaldeans, Phœnicians, Babylonians, and Persians, the Aryan philosophers of India had already discovered the evolution of the universe out of one eternal Energy, and of man from the lower animals.

Many people have an idea that India is inhabited by idolatrous heathens, who have neither philosophy, ethics, science, nor religion, and that whatever they possess they have acquired from the Christian missionaries; but, since the Parliament of Religions at the World's Fair in

---

* According to the best authorities of the present day, Moses lived about the fourteenth century B.C. Dr. Kuenen says: "The exodus is accordingly placed by one in B.C. 1321, by another in B.C. 1320, and by a third in 1314 B.C. Of course, perfect accuracy on this point is unattainable. With this reservation I accept the year 1320 B.C. as the most probable."—Religion of Israel, Vol. I, p. 121.

Chicago in 1893, the educated men and women of this country have cast aside all such erroneous notions. They have learned, on the contrary, that India has always been the fountain-head of every system of philosophy, and the home of all the religious thought of the world. The majority of Oriental scholars, like Professor Max Müller and Professor Paul Deussen, as also advanced students in America, have now come to realize that from ancient times India has produced a nation of philosophers, and that all the phases of philosophic thought, whether ancient or modern, can still be found there to-day. Victor Cousin, the eminent French philosopher, whose knowledge of the history of European philosophy was unrivalled, writes: "When we read the poetical and philosophical monuments of the East,—above all, those of India, which are beginning to spread in Europe, —we discover there many a truth, and truths so profound, and which make such a contrast with the meanness of the results at which the European genius has sometimes stopped, that we are constrained to bend the knee before the philosophy of the East, and to see in this cradle of the human race the native land of the highest philosophy." * And elsewhere he declares that "India contains the whole history of philosophy in a nutshell."

You will find no other country in the world where, from prehistoric times down to the present day, philosophy and religion have played so important a part in forming the character of the nation as they have done in India. India is the only country where, at least two thousand years before the Christian era, public assemblies, philosophic conventions, and religious congresses were held under the auspices of the reigning monarchs; and in these active part was taken, not only by priests, philosophers, and scientists, but by kings, military commanders, soldiers, merchants, peasants, and educated women of the higher classes. As early as the Vedic period, which dates from 5000 to 2000 B.C., the ancient Seers of Truth asked the most vital questions, and discussed problems that have troubled the

---

* Works, Vol. I, p. 32.

minds of the great philosophers of all ages. In those questions we can discern the development of their intellectual powers, and their insight into the true nature of things. They inquired: "When death swallows the whole world, who is the deity which shall swallow death? What part of man exists after death? What becomes of the vital forces when a man dies? What is the nature of the soul? Where is the foundation and support of this universe? What is the essence of being? What is there that governs all things and yet is separate from everything?" In trying to answer these and other problems of similar nature, the ancient thinkers discovered the laws of thought and traced the causes of phenomena, applying the rules of logic and reason at every step.

This was the beginning of philosophy in India. The minds of those truth-seekers were absolutely free from all limitations of doctrines, dogmas, and creeds. They never asked what their belief was, or whether they had faith in a personal God; but the burning questions for them were, how to acquire true knowledge of the universe, of its origin and cause, how to know the real nature of their souls, and how to solve the problems of life and death. At that time philosophic and religious thought began to ferment as actively and universally in the atmosphere of India as we find to-day in Western countries. Some of the answers given to these questions by the unbiassed thinkers of those days are truly astounding; it seems as though the ancient Seers of Truth had anticipated the conclusions of Plato, Spinoza, Berkeley, Hume, Hegel, Schopenhauer, Herbert Spencer, Haeckel, even centuries before their existence.

During the pre-Buddhistic period, or before the sixth century B.C., India gave rise to a great variety of philosophical systems, some of which were atheistic, agnostic, nihilistic, materialistic, while others were pluralistic, dualistic, or monotheistic, qualified non-dualistic, idealistic, spiritualistic, monistic systems of thought, such as are common in Europe and America at the present time. In fact, the natural tendency of the Hindu mind from the very beginning was to search after the unchangeable Reality of the universe, to trace the source of all phenomena, to understand the purpose of earthly existence, and, above all, to know what relation the individual soul bears to the Universal Being. Animated by an intense longing and guided by unswerving love for Truth, the ancient thinkers discovered many of the natural laws, and rationally explained them, without fearing contradiction or persecution; for freedom of thought has always prevailed among all classes of people in India.

These sages understood the process of cosmic evolution from a homogeneous mass into the variety of phenomena, and rejected the theory of special creation out of nothing. In one of the Upanishads we read that a sage, after explaining the mystery of Creation to his son, said: "My dear child, some people think that this world has come out of nothing, but how can something come out of nothing?" Thus we see that, unlike the Hebrews, the Hindu thinkers did not believe in special creation, but from ancient times maintained the theory of gradual evolution. It has often been remarked that the doctrine of evolution is the marvel of modern times, and that it was unknown in the past ages, but the students of Oriental literature are well aware that it was well known to the Hindus of the Vedic ages. Professor Huxley admits this when he says: "To say nothing of Indian sages, to whom evolution was a familiar notion ages before Paul of Tarsus was born." * And Sir Monier Monier Williams, in his "Brâhminism and Hinduism," declares: "Indeed, if I may be allowed the anachronism, the Hindus were Spinozites more than two thousand years before the existence of Spinoza; and Darwinians many centuries before Darwin; and evolutionists many centuries before the doctrine of evolution had been accepted by the scientists of our time, and before any word like 'evolution' existed in any language of the world." This statement is absolutely correct. If we study the philosophical systems of the great thinkers and Seers of Truth of ancient India, we shall find the most wonderful discoveries that have ever been recorded in the whole history of philosophy.

* Science and Hebrew Tradition, p. 150.

In their attempts to solve the mysteries of the phenomenal world, Hindu Seers of Truth developed six principal systems of philosophy, each having numerous branches of its own. One school traces the origin of the universe to the combination of atoms and molecules. It is known as the Vaisheshika philosophy of Kanâda. The system of Kanâda divides the phenomenal universe into six Padârthas, or categories, which embrace the whole realm of knowledge. They are these: (1) Dravya, or substance; (2) Guna, or quality; (3) Karma, or action; (4) Sâmânya, or that which constitutes a genus; (5) Vishesha, or that which constitutes the individuality or separateness of an object; and (6) Samavâya, coherence or inseparability. According to some, Abhâva, or non-existence, is the seventh substance.

Each of these, again, is subdivided into various classes. There are, for instance, nine substances: (1) earth; (2) water; (3) light; (4) air; (5) ether; (6) time (Kâla); (7) space (Dish); (8) self (Atman); and (9) mind (Manas). These substances, again, cannot exist without qualities, of which there are seventeen: color, taste, smell, touch, number (that by which we perceive one or many), extension or quantity, individuality, conjunction, priority, posteriority, thought, pleasure, pain, desire, aversion, and will. The substances are affected by five kinds of action: (1) upward motion, (2) downward motion, (3) contraction, (4) expansion, (5) movement from one spot to another. All the objects of knowledge must be either substance, quality, or motion.

According to Kanâda, the first four substances are non-eternal as aggregates, but are made up of minute invisible atoms (anus) which are eternal. They exist as inorganic and organic matter, or as instruments of sense-perceptions. Kanâda describes atoms (anus) as indivisible particles of matter which possess no visible dimensions. On this point he agrees more with modern European scientists than with Greek philosophers, who gave visible dimensions to atoms. The first aggregate of these atoms is of two (anus). It is called Dyanu, or molecule, which is still invisible. The aggregate of three molecules or double atoms forms a Trasarenu, which has visible dimension. These aggregates of composite atoms are destructible, while single atoms are indestructible by nature. How remarkable it is to see that the conception of atoms and molecules arose in India centuries before the time of Empedocles and Democritus! And the latest atomic theory of European science has not in any way surpassed that of ancient India.

Furthermore, the Vaisheshika system maintains that these atoms are not created by God, but are co-eternal with Him. The power, however, which combines two atoms and makes aggregates of atoms, comes from God, who is personal, who possesses knowledge, desire, and will, and who is the one Lord and Governor of all phenomena. According to this system, ether, time, space, Atman or Self, and mind or Manas, are eternal substances of nature. Mind or Manas is described as infinitely small, like an atom (anus); but it is distinct from Atman or Self, which is vast (Vibhu). Although mind and Atman or Self are eternal, still they are innumerable. The Self or Atman is distinct from the senses, and possesses nine qualities, such as knowledge, will, desire, happiness, etc. The aim of the Vaisheshika philosophy (which derives its name from Vishesha, the fifth substance) is the attainment of perfection and absolute freedom of the soul through the right knowledge of the causes of the phenomenal universe.

Next to the Vaisheshika is the Nyâya philosophy of Gautama. Although it is generally called a system of lògic, still it is both lcgic and philosophy. Its object is the same as other Hindu systems, namely, the true knowledge of nature, soul and God, and the attainment of ultimate freedom. This system, although based upon the atomic theory of Kanâda, begins with the enumeration of sixteen Padârthas, or subjects for discussion: (1) Pramâna, proof or means of knowledge; (2) Prameya, or objects of knowledge; (3) Sansaya, or doubt; (4) Prayojana, motive or purpose; (5) Dristânta, example or instance; (6) Siddhânta, or determined truth; (7) Avayava, syllogism or premisses; (8) Tarka, reasoning or confutation; (9) Nirnaya, or conclusion; (10) Vâda, or argumentation; (11) Jalpa, or sophistry; (12) Vitandâ, objection; (13) Hetvâbhâsa, or fallacies; (14) Chhala, quibble or perversion; (15) Jâti, or false analogies; and, (16) Nigrahasthâna, or unfitness for arguing. The correct knowledge of each of these is the aim of this school. According to Gautama, the means of knowledge are four: (1) sensuous perception; (2) inference; (3) analogy; (4) Shabda, or verbal testimony.

The objects of knowledge are twelve in number: Self or Atman, body, organs of senses, objective perception, intellect (Buddhi), mind (Manas), will, fault, state after death, retribution, pain, and final emancipation. These objects, as well as the means of knowledge, which are described singly and elaborately, form the fundamental principles of the philosophy of Nyâya, while the rest of the Padârthas belong to the system of logic which it expounds. Therefore it is both logic and philosophy. Gautama is called the Aristotle of India. He was the founder of Hindu logic, which has gradually developed into a perfect logical system, and to which have been added voluminous works by the best Hindu logicians of later date. The principal aim of Gautama's system was to establish right methods of reasoning, and to develop correct inference by the construction of true syllogisms. The Hindu syllogism consists of five parts: (1) proposition, (2) reason, (3) instance, (4) application of the reason, and (5) conclusion. By omitting two parts of this, we can make it a perfect syllogism of Aristotle. The connection in the major premiss of Aristotle's syllogism is called in Hindu logic *Vyâpti*, or invariable concomitance. Speaking of Hindu logic, Mr. Davies says: "The right methods of reasoning have been discussed with as much subtlety as by any of the Western logicians." Many European scholars, after finding a close resemblance between the logic of Aristotle and that of Gautama, have arrived at the conclusion that perhaps the Greeks borrowed the first elements of their logic and philosophy from the Hindus. Mr. Dutt says: "Comparing dates, we are disposed to say of this as of many other sciences, The Hindus invented logic, the Greeks perfected it." * We must not forget the historical fact that there was a close intercourse between the Greeks and the Hindus from the time of Pythagoras, who, it is said, went to India to gather the wisdom of the Hindus. Alexander himself was so deeply impressed, when he heard about the Hindu philosophers, that he desired to make their acquaintance. It is also said that he brought many Hindu philosophers back to Greece with him. These two schools of philosophy, the Vaisheshika and the Nyâya, supplement each other, and have at present many followers in some parts of India, especially in Bengal and among the Jains.

Then comes the Sânkhya system of Kapila. Kapila lived about 700 B.C. He is called the father of the evolution theory in India. His system is more like the philosophy of Herbert Spencer. He rejected the atomic theory by tracing the origin of atoms to one eternal cosmic energy, which he called *Prakriti* (Latin, *Procreatrix*, the creative energy). He main-

* Civilization in Ancient India, Vol. I, p. 292.

tained that the whole phenomenal universe has evolved out of one cosmic energy which is eternal. Kapila defined atoms as force centers, which correspond to the *Ions* and *Electrons* of modern science. It was Kapila who for the first time explained creation as the result of attraction and repulsion, which literally means love and hatred of atoms, as Empedocles puts it.

The Sânkya philosophy of Kapila, in short, is devoted entirely to the systematic, logical, and scientific explanation of the process of cosmic evolution from that primordial Prakriti, or eternal Energy. There is no ancient philosophy in the world which was not indebted to the Sânkhya system of Kapila. The idea of evolution which the ancient Greeks and neo-Platonists had can be traced back to the influence of this Sânkhya school of thought. Professor E. W. Hopkins says: "Plato is full of Sânkhyan thought, worked out by him, but taken from Pythagoras. Before the sixth century B.C. all the religious-philosophical ideas of Pythagoras are current in India (L. Schroeder, *Pythagoras*). If there were but one or two of these cases, they might be set aside as accidental coincidences, but such coincidences are too numerous to be the result of chance." And again he writes: "Neo-Platonism and Christian Gnosticism owe much to India. The Gnostic ideas in regard to a plurality of heavens and spiritual worlds go back directly to Hindu sources. Soul and light are one in the Sânkhya system, before they became so in Greece, and when they appear united in Greece it is by means of the thought which is borrowed from India. The famous three qualities of the Sânkhya reappear as the Gnostic 'three classes.'"*

In his "Hindu Philosophy," John Davies speaks of Kapila's system as the first recorded system of philosophy in the world, and calls it "the earliest attempt on record to give an answer, from reason alone, to the mysterious questions which arise in every thoughtful mind about the origin of the world, the nature and relations of man and his future destiny." Furthermore, Mr. Davies says, in reference to the German philosophy of Schopenhauer and of Hartmann, that it is "a reproduction of the

* Religions of India, pp. 559, 560.

philosophic system of Kapila in its materialistic part, presented in a more elaborate form, but on the same fundamental lines. In this respect the human intellect has gone over the same ground that it occupied more than two thousand years ago; but on a more important question it has taken a step in retreat. Kapila recognized fully the existence of a soul in man, forming indeed his proper nature,—the absolute of Fichte,—distinct from matter and immortal; but our latest philosophy, both here and in Germany, can see in man only a highly developed organization." *

It is most startling to find that the ultimate conclusions of this Sânkhya system harmonize and coincide with those of modern science. It says: (1) Something cannot come out of nothing; (2) The effect lies in the cause, that is, the effect is the cause reproduced; (3) Destruction means the reversion of an effect to its causal state; (4) The laws of nature are uniform and regular throughout; (5) The building up of the cosmos is the result of the evolution

* Preface to Hindu Philosophy.

of the cosmic energy. These are some of the conclusions which Kapila arrived at through observation and experiment, and by following strictly the rules of inductive logic.

Kapila denied the existence of a Creator; but still his philosophy is not considered atheistic, because he admitted the existence of the individual soul, Purusha, as an eternal and immortal entity. The different schools of Buddhistic philosophy are based upon the Sânkhya system of Kapila. The agnosticism of the Jain philosophy, which has now a large number of followers in India, is also based upon the truths of this system; while the main principles of the Sânkhya teachings have played a most important part in the popular forms of the symbol-worship of modern India.

Next in order comes the Yoga philosophy of Patanjali. Patanjali accepts the theory of evolution as explained by Kapila, and maintains that the whole phenomenal universe is the result of the evolution of Prakriti, the eternal Energy. Like Kapila, Patanjali believes in the existence of countless Purushas, or individual souls, each of which is by nature eternal, infinite, and immortal. But this system differs from Sânkhya by admitting the existence of a cosmic Purusha (personal God), who is formless, infinite, omniscient, and untouched by affliction, activity, deserts, and desires. Patanjali takes up the psychology of Sânkhya, and explains most elaborately the various functions of the *Chitta*, or mind-substance. Both Kapila and Patanjali maintain that mind-substance is material,—that it is the product of the insentient Prakriti. On this point they anticipated the conclus'ons of the materialistic philosophers of modern Europe; but they admitted that mind-substance, or Chitta, is distinct from Purusha, or true Self, which is the source of consciousness and intelligence.

The Yoga system devotes itself to the higher psychology of the human mind. It divides Chitta into five classes of *Vrittis*, or modifications: Right knowledge, indiscrimination, verbal delusion, sleep, memory.* Right knowledge proceeds from direct sensuous perception, inference, and com-

* *Vide* "Râja Yoga," by Swâmi Vivekânanda, p. 109.

petent evidence. These and various other mental functions are minutely described by Patanjali. After explaining all the modifications of the Chitta, Patanjali shows the method by which absolute control over mind (*Manas*), intellect (*Buddhi*), Chitta, and egotism (*Ahankâra*) can be attained. For the highest aim of his philosophy is to separate the Purusha from Prakriti, with which it is at present closely related; and to make it reach *Kaivalya*, or final emancipation from the bondage of nature and its qualities.

Patanjali also explains the science of concentration and meditation, the science of breath, clairaudience, telepathy, and various other psychic powers, and shows the way by which one can attain to God-consciousness in this life. There is no system of psychological philosophy in the world so complete as the psychology of Patanjali. The modern psychology of Europe, strictly speaking, is not true psychology, because it does not admit the existence of *Psyche*, the soul; as Schopenhauer says: "The study of psychology is vain, for there is no Psyche." It may be called physiological psychology, or *somatology*, as my friend, Professor Hiram Corson, of Cornell University, calls it. True psychology you will find to-day in the Yoga system of Patanjali. This philosophy has still many followers in different parts of India.

There is yet another school of philosophy, called the *Purva Mimânsa* of Jaimini. The word "Mimânsa" means investigation, and "Purva" means former or prior. This system examines the various injunctions of the ritualistic portion of the Vedas (Karma Kânda), and points out that the highest duty of man is to follow those injunctions as strictly as possible, for they are the direct revelation of the Supreme Being. According to Jaimini, the words of the Vedas are eternal, and the relation of these words to their meaning is also eternal; so the Vedas had no human origin. This system of philosophy explains the authoritative sources of knowledge, the relation between word and thought, and how this world is the manifestation of the word. We see a cow because there is in the Vedas such a word as "cow" (in the Sanskrit *Gau*). If the word cow did not exist, the material object as cow would be non-existent. We may laugh at such conclusions at present, but when we go deep into the subject and try to understand the relation which lies between thought and word, we shall realize the truth of such statements. The sun exists because there is the word "sun" in the Vedas; that is, the sun is nothing but a part of the manifestation of that *Logos* or eternal thought form which exists in the cosmic mind.

Purva Mimânsa may also be called the philosophy of work. It describes the true nature of duty and of daily works, sacrificial, ritualistic, and devotional. Through it we can understand which is right work and in what way it should be performed to produce certain results. For instance, if we wish to go to heaven we shall have to perform certain acts and those acts will create a certain unknown or imperceptible result, which will be rewarded or manifested in the form of our going to heaven. Now, how do these things happen? What is the law? And if we perform that very act in some other way, what defects would be produced in the result? All these minute points are discussed. You may throw them away as speculation, but those who believe in the efficacy of prayers, in the law of action and reaction, of cause and sequence, cannot reject them as mere speculation, because there is some truth in them. We cannot deny it. Every thought that we think or every movement of the body that we make, must produce some result somewhere in some form. What are those results? How will they affect our being? We are too busy to think of these subtle problems now, but there are thinkers who can explain a great deal on these higher and finer lines of nature. Referring to the logic of this system, Professor Colebrook says: "Each case is examined and determined upon general principles, and from the cases decided the principles may be collected. A well-ordered arrangement of them would constitute the philosophy of law; and this is, in truth, what has been attempted in the Mimânsa." This being an orthodox philosophy, it appeals to the students of the Vedas, and especially to the Brâhmin priests.

Lastly comes the *Uttara Mimânsa,* or the

system of Vedanta. This is the most popular philosophy of India to-day. Since the decline of Buddhistic philosophy in India, Vedanta has become most prominent and most powerful, having a large following among all classes of people, from the priests down to the pariahs. Among the six schools, the Vedanta philosophy has reached the highest pinnacle of philosophic thought which the human mind can possibly attain. A careful study of these different systems shows that they contain all the highest truths which were known to the ancient Greek philosophers of the Pythagorean and Eleatic schools. Professor E. W. Hopkins says: "Both Thales and Parmenides were indeed anticipated by Hindu sages, and the Eleatic school seems to be but a reflection of the Upanishads. The doctrines of Anaxamander and Heraclitus were perhaps not known first in Greece." * Frederic Schlegel writes: "The divine origin of man, as taught by the Vedanta, is continually inculcated, to stimulate his efforts to return, to animate him in the struggle, and incite him to consider a

* Religions of India.

reunion and reincorporation with Divinity as the one primary object of every action and reaction. Even the loftiest philosophy of the Europeans, the idealism of reason as it is set forth by the Greek philosophers, appears in comparison with the abundant light and vigor of Oriental idealism like a feeble Promethean spark in the full flood of heavenly glory of the noonday sun, faltering and feeble and ever ready to be extinguished." *

The ultimate reality of the universe, according to Vedanta, is the one Absolute Substance which is beyond subject and object, which is the infinite source of intelligence or knowledge, of consciousness and blissfulness, which is one and not many. It is called in Sanskrit *Brahman*. It is the same as the Good of Plato, the "Ding-an-sich" or the transcendental Thing-in-itself of Kant, the Will of Schopenhauer, the *Substantia* of Spinoza, the Over-Soul of Emerson, the Unknowable of Herbert Spencer, the Divine Essence of the Heavenly Father of the Christians, and of Allah of the Mahometans. It is also the true nature of Buddha and of Christ. It pervades the uni-

* Indian Language, Literature, and Philosophy, p. 471.

verse. It is one and universal. No one can divide it: it is indivisible. This is the reality of the universe, says Vedanta.

The system of Vedanta is more critical than the Kantian system, because it shows the phenomenal nature of the Kantian ego, of his forms of intuition, and his categories of thought. It is also more sublime than the philosophy of Kant, because it recognizes and proves the identity of the objective reality of the universe with the subjective reality of the ego. Kant did not realize that the Thing-in-itself ("Ding-an-sich") of the objective world and the "Ding-an-sich" of the subjective world are one. In no other system of philosophy has this oneness been so clearly explained and so strongly emphasized as it is in Vedanta. Professor Max Müller says: "This constitutes the unique character of Vedanta, unique compared with every other philosophy of the world which has not been influenced by it, directly or indirectly." * There have been many European philosophies which have denied the existence of the external world, but not one

* The Six Systems of Indian Philosophy, p. 223.

of them has ventured to deny the apparent reality of the ego, of the senses, of the mind, and of their inherent forms. In this respect Vedanta holds a most unique position among the philosophies of the world. After lifting the Self or the true nature of the ego, Vedanta unites it with the essence of Divinity, which is absolutely pure, perfect, immortal, unchangeable, and one. No philosopher, not even Plato, Spinoza, Kant, Hegel, or Schopenhauer, has reached that height of philosophic thought. Professor Max Müller declares: "None of our philosophers, not excepting Heraclitus, Plato, Kant, or Hegel, has ventured to erect such a spire, never frightened by storms or lightnings. Stone follows on stone, in regular succession after once the first step has been made, after once it has been clearly seen that in the beginning there can have been but One, as there will be but One in the end, whether we call it Atman or Brahman." *

Although Vedanta has united heaven and earth, God and man, Brahman and Atman, still it has destroyed nothing in the phenomenal

* The Six Systems of Indian Philosophy, p. 239.

world. It accepts all the ultimate conclusions of modern science; but at the same time it says that Truth is one and not many, yet there can be many expressions and various manifestations of the one Truth. Furthermore, it maintains that the aim of the higher philosophy is not merely to ascertain the established conjunctions of events which constitute the order of the universe, or to record the phenomena which it exhibits to our observation and refer them to the general laws, but also to lead the human mind from the realm of the knowable to that which is beyond the knowable. We are now living in the realm of the knowable; but that which teaches simply the laws which govern the knowable phenomena is not the highest kind of philosophy. We must know the laws of the knowable, yet at the same time we should aspire to go beyond the knowable and plunge into the realm of the Infinite. If any philosophy can help us in this attempt, then it must be higher than the ordinary system which keeps us within the limits of the knowable. Vedanta philosophy guides us above all knowable objects of perception, and directs our souls toward the Eternal Absolute Being, wherein we find the solution of all problems and the answer to all questions. Its attempt is to trace the relation between the soul and God, not by any unscientific method, but by the most rigorous processes of logic and reason, starting from the ultimate generalizations of the various branches of science.

True philosophy must construct a theory which will be the simplest in its nature, and yet at the same time will explain all the vital problems which the science of the phenomenal-knowable can never explain, and which will harmonize with the highest form of universal religion, without destroying the loftiest aspirations of the human soul. True philosophy in the widest sense must perform three great functions. First, it must coördinate the ultimate results arrived at by special branches of knowledge which we call sciences, and, taking up those conclusions, it must form the widest generalizations possible. When it does this, it is called phenomenology. Herbert Spencer's philosophy performs this function most wonderfully, but it leaves out the vital problems which perplex the minds of the greatest philosophers as unsolvable mysteries. Herbert Spencer does not explain all these problems, but without finding their true solution our lives will not be worth living. We must find an explanation, we must solve all the problems which disturb the peace of our souls; and if any system will help us, we will study it, follow its teachings, and satisfy our questioning minds. Secondly, true philosophy must investigate the realm of knowledge and trace its source. You know that you are sitting here and listening: where does this knowledge come from? The minds of even the greatest thinkers have become confused in trying to answer this question. A philosophy which does this is called Epistomology. The philosophy of Kant, Hegel, Fichte, and others has performed this function. In his "Elements of General Philosophy" George Croom Robertson says: "Epistomology is just philosophy, because it deals with things, deals with being; it deals with things going beyond bare experience, but it treats of them in relation to the fact of knowing. Thus an epistomologist cannot help being an ontologist, because his theory of knowledge must treat about things also as being. He must also be a metaphysician, because he is concerned with the whole range of things beyond the physical; he must be a philosopher in being other and more than a man of science, or concerned with things in a way in which science is not." Science, with its various branches, directs us up to a certain point, and cannot go further; but where science ends, there is the beginning of true philosophy. The third function which true philosophy performs is that of leading our minds into the realm of the Absolute, of the Unknown, and then it solves the problems of life and death. It explains the origin of the universe and of individual existence, and the purpose of evolution. On the plane of relativity the perfect solution of these vital problems can never be found. Furthermore, when this phase of true philosophy directs our minds toward the Infinite, it helps us in becoming free from all limitations of ignorance and selfishness. These limitations are the greatest bondage that we are now suffering from, and, by performing this function, true philosophy lays the foundation of the highest form of monistic religion. No philosophy in the world performs these three functions so satisfactorily as Vedanta. Hence we may say that Vedanta is the most complete of all systems.

Philosophy and religion must always be in perfect harmony. Ernest Haeckel, in his "Riddle of the Universe," tries to give a foundation to monistic religion; but his monism is one-sided, because he says that the ultimate substance of the universe is unintelligent. His insentient substance may be compared with Kapila's Prakriti, which is eternal and unintelligent. According to Vedanta, however, the final substance of the universe is Brahman, which is *Sat* or absolute existence, *Chit* or absolute intelligence, and *Ananda* or absolute bliss. Vedanta teaches that that which is the substance of our souls must possess intelligence, consciousness, and blissfulness. Thus Vedanta lays the true foundation of a universal religion which is monistic or non-dualistic. The monistic religion of Vedanta does not admit the Sânkhyan theory of the plurality of Purushas, or individual souls, which are eternal and infinite by nature, but on the contrary, by following the strict rules of logic, it establishes that the Infinite must be one and not many. From one many have come into existence, and the individual souls are but so many images or reflections of the Absolute Brahman. It teaches that the true nature of the soul is Divine. From the Absolute Brahman the phenomenal universe rises, and in the end returns into the Brahman. The religion of Vedanta admits the existence of *Iswara*, the personal God, who is the first-born Lord of the universe, who starts the evolution of Prakriti, who loves all living creatures and can be loved and worshipped in return. In Vedanta the Prakriti of the Sânkhya philosophy is called Mâyâ, which is the divine energy of the Absolute Brahman. Mâyâ does not mean illusion, as some scholars think; but it is that power which produces time, space, and causation, as also the phenomenal appearances which exist on the relative plane. Thus we see that the system of Vedanta is both philosophy and religion. Of the tree of knowledge, philosophy is the flower and religion is the fruit, so they must go together. Religion is nothing but the practical side of philsophy, and philosophy is the theoretical side of religion.

In India a true philosopher is not a mere speculator but a spiritual man. He does not believe in certain theories which cannot be carried into practice in every-day life; what he believes he lives, and therefore practical philosophy is still to be found in India. For example, an Indian philosopher who follows Kanâda, and believes in the existence of a personal God as the essence of his soul, does not merely accept this theoretically, but he tries to realize it in his daily life. A Buddhist, again, will explain all the most abstruse problems, and at the same time you will see that he is living out his beliefs. So with a follower of the Sânkhya system, or of Vedanta: they are not mere speculative philosophers, but they live spiritual lives and strive to attain God-consciousness. In India, if any one writes voluminous works and leads a worldly life, he is not considered a true philosopher; but in the West a man can become a philosopher by simply sitting in his library and writing a book, although his every-day life may be far from spiritual.

A friend of mine, being asked whether India had produced a philosopher like Ralph Waldo Emerson, replied: "America has produced one Emerson, but in India you will find an Emerson every five miles." This is not a great exaggeration, and the reason, as I have already said, is that the Hindus not only theorize but live philosophy. Hindu minds are extremely logical. They will not accept any theory which does not harmonize with logic and reason. Therefore you will scarcely find an irrational doctrine or dogma in the religion of Vedanta. Freedom of thought, as I have already said, has always prevailed in India since the Vedic period. For this reason Christian missionaries meet with the greatest opposition when they preach to the Hindus the unscientific and illogical doctrines and dogmas of their faith. When, for instance, they try to teach them the creation of the universe in six days as given in Genesis, the Hindus smile at the missionaries and reject their statements as unscientific and irrational. Similarly they will not listen to other Christian dogmas, like infant damnation, eternal perdition of the heathen, etc.

The philosophy and religion of Vedanta embrace all the sciences and philosophies of the world, accepting their latest conclusions, and classify them according to their order of merit. Consequently the universality of Vedanta is unique and unparalleled. In this system the people of India find the ultimate truths of all sciences, of all philosophies, as well as of all religions. It is so popular because it solves the problems concerning the origin and final aim of earthly life, fulfils the highest aspiration of human souls, and inculcates that the true nature of the soul is immortal by its birthright. Vedanta maintains that, if the soul were mortal by nature, it could never become immortal, for that which could be made immortal could be unmade. This is an argument which cannot be refuted, and it has taken such hold of the logical mind of the Hindus that, even when they are converted to other faiths, they cannot believe that the soul, which is by nature a child of God, can ever be made immortal by Christ.

Vedanta has the largest following, and is the prevailing philosophy of India to-day. Since the eighth century A.D., when, after the decline of Buddhism, it was revived by the earnest efforts of its commentator, Sri Sankarâchârya, who is now regarded as the greatest philosopher of the world, the Vedanta philosophy has taken firm root in the remotest corner of every Hindu community, from the highest to the lowest, and has overshadowed all other systems of philosophic thought. Professor Max Müller, in the preface to his "Six Systems of Philosophy," writes: "Other philosophies do exist and have some following, but Vedanta has the largest"; and he also affirms that Vedanta is both a philosophy and a religion by saying: "For all practical purposes, the Vedantist would hold that the whole phenomenal world, both in its subjective and objective character, should be accepted as real. It is as real as anything can be to the ordinary mind; it is not mere emptiness, as the Buddhists maintain. And thus the Vedanta philosophy leaves to every man a wide sphere of real usefulness, and places him under a law as strict and binding as anything can be in this transitory life; it leaves him a Deity to worship as omnipotent and majestic as the deities of any other religion. It has room for almost every religion; nay, it embraces them all." *

* Three Lectures on Vedanta Philosophy.

II.

THE RELIGION OF INDIA TO-DAY.

FEW people realize the vastness of India. If we include British Burmah, it is as large in area as the whole of Europe except Russia, or nearly two-thirds of the United States, with a population almost three and a half times as great. It is a country with a vast conglomeration of nations and languages, far more diverse than in America or in any other country of the world. Among this huge mass of inhabitants we find the followers of every great religion; there are Christians, Mahometans, Jews, Parsees or Zoroastrians, Buddhists, Jains, Sikhs, and Hindus. According to the census of 1901 the adherents of the different faiths in India number as follows:

Christians	2,923,241
Mahometans	62,458,077
Jews	18,228
Parsees	94,190
Buddhists (chiefly in Burmah)	9,476,759
Jains	1,334,148
Sikhs	2,195,339
Hindus	207,147,026

The Jews are scattered in large cities like Bombay, Poona, and Calcutta. The Parsees are to be found in the Bombay Presidency; but in India proper there are very few Buddhists. Besides these, there are about six hundred thousand Aboriginal non-Aryans who are ancestor or spirit-worshippers. The majority of the population are known as Hindus and their religion is called Hinduism. The words "Hindu" and "Hinduism," however, are entirely of foreign origin. In ancient times, when the Persians and Greeks invaded India, they came across a river in the northwest of India which was called in Sanskrit "Sindhu" (the Indus of modern geography), but, in Zend and in Greek, "Hindu." Consequently, those who inhabited the banks of the "Sindhu" or Indus were named by the Greeks and Persians " Hindus " and their land "Hindustan." If we remember this derivation we shall be able to understand why these words "Hindu" and "Hinduism" do not mean anything to the natives of India, who call themselves, not Hindus, but Aryas or Aryans. The inhabitants of India to-day are the descendants of the same Aryan family from which the Anglo-Saxons, Germans, and Latin races have descended. They came originally from Central Asia,—some say from the North Pole and others from Europe; but we do not know the exact spot where the ancient forefathers of the Aryans lived.

The word "Hindu," therefore, refers to the descendants of the Indo-Aryans who at present inhabit India and call themselves Aryas or Aryans; while their religion is known among themselves as "Arya-Dharma" (the religion of the Aryans), or "Sanâtana-Dharma," which means "that religion which lasts throughout eternity," for, according to the Hindus, this religion is eternal. It has always existed, and will continue as long as the world will exist.

Some people may think that it is a natural religion; but if we trace the origin of all so-called supernatural religions, we shall find that they were in some way connected with India, the home of all the religious systems of the world, and that, when other countries and other nations had no religion at all, the eternal religion of the Hindus not only prevailed but was fully developed.

Under the name of Hinduism there still exists in India to-day a system of religion which embraces all the religious thought of the world. It stands like a huge banyan-tree, spreading its far-reaching branches over hundreds of sects, creeds, and denominations, and covering with its innumerable leaves all forms of worship,—the dualistic, qualified non-dualistic, and monistic worship of the One Supreme God, the worship of the Incarnation of God, and also hero-worship, saint-worship, symbol-worship, ancestor-worship, and the worship of departed spirits. It is based upon the grand idea of universal receptivity. It receives everything. It is like an immense hospitable mansion which welcomes all worshippers, from the lowest to the highest, all believers in the existence of God, and which has never refused admission to any sincere applicant for spiritual freedom. The prevailing religion of India may be compared to a vast mosaic, inlaid with every kind of religious idea and every form of worship which the human mind can possibly conceive. If any one wishes to study the history of the gradual evolution of the worship of the One Supreme Being step by step, from its lowest to its highest phase, let him go to India and study the living history of religions. Let him simply watch the lives of the followers of existing sects, for Professor Max Müller says: "No phase of religion, from the coarsest superstition to the most sublime enlightenment, is unrepresented in that country."

This universal religion, strictly speaking, is neither Hinduism nor Brâhminism, although it has been called both, as well as by still other names. But why should we call it Brâhminism? The term, which is an invention of the Christian missionaries, has no meaning to the Hindus, because no Brâhmin was its founder. This eternal religion, indeed, is nameless and it had no founder. Zoroastrianism, Judaism, Christianity, Mahometanism, had their founders and were built around the personality of these founders; but the religion of the Hindus is not limited by any book, or by the existence or non-existence of any particular person. If we study the words of the earliest-known Rishi, or Vedic "Seer of Truth," even he alludes to others who had seen similar truths before him. It is for this reason that the religion of the Indo-Aryans never had any special creed or dogma or theology as its guide. Everything that harmonized with the eternal laws described by the ancient Seers of Truth was recognized and accepted by them as true.

From the very beginning this religion has been as free as the air which we breathe. As air touches all flowers and carries their fragrance along with it wherever it blows, so the Sanâtana religion takes in all that is true and beneficial to mankind. Like the sky overhead, it embraces the spiritual atmosphere around all nations and all countries. It is a well-known fact that this eternal religion of the Hindus surpasses Zoroastrianism, Judaism, Christianity, and Mahometanism in its antiquity, grandeur, sublimity, and, above all, in its conception of God. The God of the Hindus is omnipresent, omnipotent, omniscient, all-merciful, and impersonally personal. He is not like the extra-cosmic Creator as described in Genesis, but is immanent and resident in nature. He is more merciful, more impartial, more just, more compassionate, than Jahveh, the tribal god of the sons of Israel. The God of the Aryan religion is more benevolent and more unlimited in power and majesty than the Ahura Mazda of the Zoroastrians. You will find monotheism at the foundation of every religious structure, and other nations do not go beyond this; but the Indian people are not satisfied to stop with monotheism; they want something higher.

The religion of the Indo-Aryans of to-day can be classified under three heads,—dualistic, qualified non-dualistic, and monistic. The first two, that is, the dualistic and qualified non-dualistic phases, have given foundation to the various sects of worshippers who are known as Vaishnavas, Shaivas, Shâktas, Gânapatyas, Sauryas; of these, the last two sects have become almost extinct at the present time. The majority of Hindus, both men and women, are either Vaishnavas, Shaivas, or Shâktas.

The Vaishnavas are those who worship the Supreme Being, the all-knowing, all-loving, and omnipotent Lord, Governor, and Protector of the universe, under the name of Vishnu. Vishnu is the name of the second person of the Hindu Trinity, the literal meaning of the word being "all-pervading," "omnipresent." According to the Hindu belief, Vishnu, or the Lord of the universe, is both personal and impersonal. In his impersonal aspect he pervades the universe, interpenetrates the atoms and molecules, and fills the infinite space like the glorious light of the self-effulgent sun. In his personal aspect he dwells in the highest heaven. The personal Lord of the universe also incarnates Himself on this earth in every age to establish the eternal religion and to help mankind. "Whenever true religion declines and irreligion prevails, says the Lord, I manifest myself to establish true religion and to destroy evil." *

Some people think that this idea of the incarnation of God was borrowed from the Christians; but it can be proved, on the contrary, that it existed in India centuries before Christ was born. In fact, India is the home of this belief, which was afterwards adopted by other religions. The Hindus maintain that since the beginning of the world God has incarnated many times, and will come again and again. They have recognized many incarnations in the past, and believe that there will be many in the future. On this point they differ from the Christians, who believe that there was only one incarnation, and that that was the first and the last. According to the Hindu faith, God can manifest in any place at any time, because His powers are unlimited. If we limit Him by saying that there has been only one incarnation, then we make Him finite; but as He is Infinite in His powers, in His glory, and in His manifestations, He ought not to be limited by time, space, or nationality. His love

* Bhagavad Gita, Ch. IV, v. 7.

for all nations is equal, and whenever and wherever His manifestation is necessary, there He naturally descends. These incarnations are called in Sanskrit Avatâras, which means the descent of the Supreme Being for the good of humanity.

Râma, the hero of the great epic Râmâyana, for instance, is regarded as one of the great incarnations of ancient India. To-day, in various parts of the country, especially in the north-western provinces and in central India, there are millions and millions of souls who worship Râma as the Saviour of mankind, who look upon him as the ideal son, the ideal king, the ideal father, and the ideal husband; who repeat his holy name with the deepest feelings of love and devotion; who chant his praises in the morning, at noon, and in the evening; who sing songs describing the exploits of this great Avatâra; who every day read a portion of the Râmâyana in Sanskrit or in Hindustanee, or in any other vernacular; and who in their daily life follow the teachings and the high moral and ethical ideals exemplified in the character of Sri Râma, the embodiment of Truth eternal. For the sake of truthfulness, Râma abandoned his throne, went into the forest, and lived there for fourteen long years, practising austerities in order to set an example of perfect truthfulness. His consort Sitâ, the noblest, purest, and most perfect ideal of womanhood that India has produced, is now the exalted spiritual ideal of every Hindu woman, old or young. Those who have read the Râmâyana will remember the unparalleled character of Sitâ, the ideal wife and mother. She was the most wonderful character that the world has ever seen. To show her faithfulness to her lord, she sacrificed everything; she was, indeed, like the personification of loyalty and purity. Hanumân, again, who is erroneously called by the Christian missionaries the monkey god, represents the ideal devotee and the perfect embodiment of faith and devotion; and whenever a worshipper of Râma thinks of these qualities, he holds Hanumân as the ideal before him. Those who worship Râma are known as Râmât Vaishnavas. They regard Râma and Vishnu as one.

Then there are many millions of Vaishnavas all over India who worship Krishna, the

Hindu Christ. Krishna is regarded as the greatest of all Avatâras or Divine Incarnations. He lived about 1400 B.C. His life, which is described in the Mahâbhârata, the history of ancient India, as also in many Purânas, resembles that of Jesus the Christ, not only in His miraculous birth, but in all the principal events of His earthly career. He was, for example, born in a cave, and at the time of his birth an Indian Herod, Kamsa by name, ordered all infants to be killed. Krishna also resuscitated the dead, brought animals back to life, and performed many other miracles. Those who have read the Bhagavad Gita, or Song Celestial, as Sir Edwin Arnold calls it, will remember how vast was the divine wisdom of the sin-atoning Krishna, the Redeemer of the world. He is regarded by all Hindus as the Saviour of mankind in the same way as Christ is in Christendom. They worship him, repeat his holy name, and chant his praises at all hours of the day, as a devout Roman Catholic saint would do.

Both Krishna and Râma are manifestations of the same Vishnu, the Lord of the universe.

This is a difficult thing for Western minds to grasp, and for that reason they think the Hindus polytheists. But they are not polytheists. They worship One God under different names and forms. Râma was the incarnation of Vishnu, and so was Krishna. In their spiritual essence they are one and the same, but in their manifestations they are different. Both have their statues in all the big temples of India, just as we see the images of Christ and Mary in the Cathedrals of Christendom. The Christian missionaries, however, not understanding the Hindu form of worship, have misrepresented these statues and called them idols. Here let me assure you that there is no such thing as idol-worship, in your sense of the term, in any part of India, not even among the most illiterate classes. I have seen more idolatry in Italy than in India. The Italian peasants even beat the Bambino when their prayers are not answered, but in India you will not find such spiritual darkness anywhere. There the people worship the *Ideal*, not the idol. Statues and figures are kept in the temples as reminders of the deeds of the great Saviours. It is the memory, the spirit, of Râma and Krishna, which the Hindus worship; but if you ask a Brâhmin priest whom he worships, or where is Krishna, he will tell you that Lord Krishna dwells everywhere; he is the Soul of our souls, the Heart of our hearts. He is not confined to any particular form made of wood or stone. Is this idolatry? If so, what kind of idolatry is it? It is very easy for any one to say that it is the worship of a false god, or of an idol; but if a person will look beneath the surface and inquire of the Hindus themselves, he can readily discover how mistaken such assertions are. If the Hindus are idol-worshippers because they show respect to their Spiritual Masters, like Krishna and Râma, why should not the Christians be called idolaters when they show respect to Christ, kneeling down before his statue or picture? If the Hindu is idolatrous because he fixes his mind on some religious symbol, like the cross or triangle or circle, why should not the same term be applied to the Christian when he thinks of the crucifix and keeps it on the altar?

Images and symbols are also used in Hindu temples as aids to the practice of concentration and meditation. This is a peculiar mode of worship common among the Hindus. There may be no outward signs of worship. A man will perhaps sit cross-legged on the floor, close his eyes, and remain as motionless as a statue: his devotion will all be internal. He will withdraw his mind from the external world and fix it upon the Supreme Being; but the starting-point of his concentration and meditation will be these symbols and figures, because the natural tendency of the mind is to go from the concrete to the abstract and then to the Absolute. So there may be many symbols in the temples; the cross, for instance. The cross was a religious symbol in India long before Christ was born. The *swastika* is the oldest of all forms of the cross, and that we have in India to-day. Then there is the triangle, which symbolizes the Hindu Trinity; the circle, which represents infinity; and there are many other symbols, all of which are considered extremely helpful to beginners in concentration and meditation.

The Hindus regard Krishna as the ideal incarnation of Divine Love. His mission was to establish Divine Love on this earth, and show that it can be manifested through all sanctified human relations. What Krishna has done in India, and how he has impressed the minds of the people, we cannot understand here. We must go to India to see that; we must go to *Mathurâ*, where Krishna was born, or to Vrindâvan, where he played as a shepherd-boy, to find how the Vaishnavas revere and worship him. The worship and devotion which we see to-day in India cannot be found in any other part of the world. I have travelled through many countries in Europe, and almost all over the United States and Canada, but I have not seen the pathos, the spiritual fire, that I have found among the Vaishnavas in India. God can be worshipped not only as the Master, but also as a friend, as a child, as a husband,—that is what they teach. They bring Him closer and closer, and make Him the closest and nearest to our being. Time will not permit me to go into the details of the method of worship which these Vaishnavas practise, but I can at least tell you that there are thousands and thousands of Hindu women who look upon Krishna, the Saviour of mankind, as their own child. They do not care for a human child; they want God as their child, and they consider themselves as the mother of Divinity. This is a unique thing. The mother of God! How much purity is required to make a woman think of herself as the mother of Divinity or of a Divine Incarnation! And this is their ideal. I am not exaggerating; I have seen with my eyes such wonderful characters, and I have seen them nowhere else.

These Vaishnavas, or worshippers of Krishna, can be subdivided into seven different denominations: The followers of Sankârâcharya, the great preacher and commentator of monistic Vedanta; the followers of Râmânuja, another great preacher and commentator, who lived in the southern part of India, and whose followers are known as qualified non-dualists; the followers of Madhvâchârya, the preacher of the dualistic school; and the followers of Chaitanya, of Ballavâchârya, of Râmânanda, and Nimbâchârya. Each of these was an ideal prophet, spiritual leader, and commentator of the philosophy of Vedanta, as also the founder of a denomination which still has millions of followers all over the country. They differ only in the minor peculiarities of their doctrines, beliefs, and modes of worship; but they all agree on one point,—that Krishna was the greatest of all Divine Incarnations, that he was the Saviour of mankind and the Redeemer of the world.

The worshippers of Krishna and of Vishnu or Râma are all vegetarians; they do not touch meat, because non-killing is their ideal. They cannot kill any animal for food. They never drink any intoxicating liquor, neither the men nor the women. That is a very difficult thing to find anywhere else. They practise non-resistance of evil, which was taught not only by Krishna, but by Buddha and afterwards by Christ. Their religion makes them loving, not only to human beings, but to all living creatures, and pure and chaste in their morals. They practise disinterested love for humanity;

they will sacrifice everything for the good of others, because their Ideal, their Master, was the sin-atoning Krishna, who sacrificed everything for the good of the world. There are no caste distinctions among the Vaishnavas. Mahometans and Pariahs have often become followers of this faith. Krishna has indeed given to earnest and sincere souls among the Hindus what Jesus the Christ has given to Christendom, and there is a great similarity in the belief and mode of worship of the Vaishnavas and those of the most devout followers of Jesus.

As the Vaishnavas regard Krishna and Râma as their Ideals, so there are Hindus who look upon other manifestations as their Ideal. The Shaivas, for example, worship Shiva, the third person of the Hindu Trinity. Shiva represents the ideal of renunciation and absolute freedom from worldliness. He is revered by the Hindus as the embodiment of contemplativeness and Yoga; he is therefore worshipped by the Yogis, saints, and sages of all sects. They repeat the name of Shiva with tears of love and devotion streaming from their eyes; they forget everything of the world when they utter his sacred name. Shiva and Vishnu, again, are one and the same in their spiritual essence; they are two manifestations of the One Infinite Being who is called Brahman in the Vedas. A Vaishnava can worship Shiva in the same spirit as he worships his own Ideal Vishnu, and a Shaiva can worship Vishnu in the same spirit as he worships his own Ideal, Shiva; because they know that He who is Vishnu is Shiva and He who is Shiva is Vishnu.

Shiva represents, as I have already said, contemplativeness, Yoga, renunciation and absolute freedom from worldliness. As Vishnu is adorned by the Vaishnavas with all blessed qualities, with all that is beautiful, all that stands for wealth, prosperity, and success in life; Shiva, on the contrary, is adorned with all that is ugly, horrible, and awe-inspiring. His beatific form is encircled by venomous snakes of evil, misfortune, and worldliness; but they cannot injure Him. Shiva dwells in the *Shmashâna*, where horrors of death and destruction surround Him, but they cannot frighten Him or disturb His blissful Samâdhi. He is the ever-undaunted conqueror of all dread, danger, passion, and distress. He is attended by ghosts and wicked spirits, but they cannot hurt Him. Shiva renounces the world for the good of humanity. Voluntarily He takes upon Himself the burdens, anxieties, sufferings, and pains of all humanity, and swallows the deadliest poison to bestow immortality upon His earnest followers and true devotees. His consort, the Divine Mother of the universe, is His only companion in austerities and penances. He lives where nobody cares to go, and He accepts the tiger-skin and the ashes from crematories as His ornaments. He is the ideal of the Yogis. If any one wishes to see and understand what renunciation means, let him go to India and study the worship of Shiva. He has many forms, many incarnations, and there are many symbols connected with His life. The Shaivas worship the snow-white form of Shiva, which symbolizes purity and freedom from all taint or worldliness, the form of Him who is the Master of the universe. Shiva can be worshipped under all circumstances. If a follower of Shiva cannot find a temple, he may sit under a tree;

he does not need any form, statue, or symbol; he simply closes his eyes and meditates upon Shiva as the Lord of the universe, beyond good and evil, beyond all relativity, the embodiment of the Infinite and Absolute Being.

The Vaishnavas and Shaivas, as we have just seen, regard the Lord of the universe as masculine and give Him masculine attributes; but there are Hindus who give to God feminine attributes and call Him the Mother of the universe. India is in fact the only place in the world where God is worshipped as the Mother, and where all women are considered as representatives of ideal Divine Motherhood. Some people think that the Hindus deny salvation to women, but no Hindu ever imagined anything so crude; on the contrary, womanhood is attributed by him to the Lord of the universe. He knows that the soul is sexless, and that it manifests on the physical plane as a man or a woman only to fulfil a certain purpose in life. The Bhagavad Gita says: "All men and women, whether they believe in God or not, are bound sooner or later to reach perfection."

Those who thus worship God as the Mother are known as Shâktas, the worshippers of Shakti, Divine Energy, the Mother of all phenomena. These Shâktas believe that the Mother of the universe manifests Her powers from time to time in human form and incarnates as a woman. There have been various feminine incarnations among the Hindus. These Divine incarnations of Shakti, or Divine Energy, are in different forms, such as Kâli, Durgâ, Târâ, etc. Foreigners cannot understand the meaning of these symbolic figures, used as aids to concentration and meditation at the time of worship, and they think, "How hideous these forms are!" Of course some of them are hideous to Western eyes, but to the Hindus they are spiritual symbols; for the people of India are not merely optimistic, they recognize both sides. They are brave. They do not deny the evil side of the world; they take that also, and adorn the Mother on the one hand with evil, murder, plague, and the most horrible things, while, on the other hand, they represent Her as overflowing with blessings and all that is good and beautiful.

Those who have only optimistic ideas shut their eyes to evils and misfortunes and curse either God or Satan when these come upon them; but among the worshippers of the Divine Mother you will find both men and women, who in time of distress face danger bravely, and pray to Her with unflinching faith and whole-hearted love, recognizing Her grandeur and Divine power even behind misfortune and calamity.

The whole truth of the Sânkhya philosophy * is symbolized in the Shakti-worship, or the worship of Divine Mother. You will remember that the Sânkhya believes in the evolution of the world and of the whole universe out of one Eternal Energy, while the individual soul is known as Purusha, the Infinite Spirit. So Shiva represents Purusha, the formless Infinite Spirit, and His consort or Shakti is that Eternal Energy, which is called in Sanskrit Prakriti. The union of the male and female principles of Divinity is the beginning of cosmic evolution. Here you will notice how the ultimate conclusions of science have been symbolized by the Hindus and

* Described in previous lecture.

made into objects of devotion and worship. Ask how the evolution of the world began and they will show you the symbol of the Purusha and Prakriti. The religion of the Hindus, in fact, embraces science, logic, and philsosophy. They think that that which is unscientific, illogical, and unphilosophical cannot be called religious, so they take the scientific truths, make symbols out of them, and, relating them to the Eternal Being, they use them as the most helpful objects for devotion and worship. The Hindu mind is very inventive along spiritual lines. It gives its inventive genius full play in the spiritual field. There is no other religion in the world which is so rich in mythology, symbology, rituals, and ceremonials, and which possesses so many phases of the Divine Ideal, as the *Sanâtana Dharma*, or the Eternal Religion of the Hindus. Its followers are freely allowed to choose their ideals in harmony with their thoughts and spiritual tendencies. They believe that one particular set of doctrines and dogmas cannot satisfy the aspirations of all human souls. As one coat cannot fit all bodies, so one particular ideal cannot fit all minds, cannot suit all the spiritual tendencies of all nations in all countries. Do we not see how Christianity has failed in that respect when it has tried to make the whole world adopt one ideal? Do we not see to-day how, among the followers of Christianity, there is a constant fight and struggle for lack of a better understanding of their religious ideal? Human minds need variety; and the paths which lead to the supreme goal should vary according to the tendency, capacity, and spiritual development of the individual. Therefore the eternal religion of the Hindus prescribes no set path, but offers various ones to suit different minds, —the path of right knowledge and right discrimination (Jnâna Yoga); of concentration and meditation (Râja Yoga); of work for work's sake (Karma Yoga); and of devotion and worship (Bhakti Yoga). Each one of these, again, has various branches. Thus we see that the Hindus alone have succeeded in giving to the world a religion which fits all minds and all tendencies under all conditions,—a religion which preaches the worship of one God, the Infinite

Being, under a variety of names and ideals. Truth is one, but its manifestations are many. This noble and sublime conception has made the Hindus extremely tolerant towards other faiths and other forms of worship outside their own; for they consider that all religions, sects, and creeds are like so many paths which lead to the same goal.

Those who do not understand the Hindu mode of thought have called it Pantheism; but it is the worship of One Universal Spirit, which is infinite, omnipotent, all-merciful, impersonal and yet personal. If you call it Pantheism, then you use the term in the wrong sense. Pantheism never means that. When I think that this table is God, or, if I consider that God has become this chair, then it will be Pantheism. But if I believe in One God, who pervades and interpenetrates the atoms and molecules of the chair and the table, or any other object of the world, then that will be the worship of the One Supreme Being, who is infinite and all-pervading.

True religion, according to the Hindus, does

not consist in belief in a certain creed or set of dogmas, but in the attainment of God-consciousness through spiritual unfoldment. It is being and becoming God. It is the subjugation of selfish love and desire for self-aggrandizement, and the expression of Divine love, truthfulness, and kindness to all. The object of such a religion is the freedom of the soul from the bondage of the world. A Hindu is not limited by sectarian doctrines and dogmas; he can go anywhere, worship any ideal that suits him and make that his chosen Ideal. As long as he believes in One God, there is no danger, he will have salvation; and this salvation can be attained in this life.

Outside of the Vaishnavas, Shaivas, and Shâktas, we find Hindus who follow other phases of religion. In the Punjab, the north-western province of India, for instance, there is a large population which is known as Sikhs. The word "Sikh" is derived from the Sanskrit "Shishya," which means "a disciple"; and the Sikhs are so called because they are disciples of their master, Guru Nânaka, who was a contemporary of Luther. Guru Nânaka was a great soul. He is regarded to-day by his disciples and followers as the manifestation of Divinity, and he left sayings and teachings. These are written out in a book, and this book the Sikhs hold in the same light as the Christians their Bible, the Mahometans their Koran, and the orthodox Hindus their Vedas. It is to them the revealed word of God. They put it upon an altar, burn incense before it, and worship it as the word of God. They cannot bear any other form or symbol or image, or the statue of any incarnation or manifestation of Divinity. They are as fanatical as the Protestant Christians in their attitude towards forms and images. They observe no caste prejudice; they are very broad and liberal-minded, and will accept the followers of any faith in their religion. At one time they converted hundreds of Mahometans and made them Sikhs. Their book is called the "Grantha-Sâhib," or the Great Scripture, and contains the most sublime moral and spiritual ideals, which harmonize with the teachings of the Vedas. They believe in One Supreme God who is formless. As the Mahometans believe in Allah, the One Formless Being, who can take no form, so these Sikhs believe in the same way. Perhaps Sikhism arose in India through the influence of Mahometanism. It is one of the recent sects.

Besides these orthodox Hindus, there are Jains and Buddhists. The Jains have their own Scriptures and their own prophets, Pârswa Nâth, Adinâth, Mahâvira Nâth, and many others, who are called *Tirthankaras* (perfected souls). These are great and immortal spiritual leaders who came down to teach mankind; any one who follows their teachings will reach absolute freedom from this world of imperfection. Jainism arose in India about the same time as Buddhism. Buddha lived about 557 B.C. He was the founder of the great religion which has civilized the larger portion of Asia, which predominates in China and Japan, which has made the Japanese a great nation, and which prevails to-day in Tibet, Siam, Burmah, Ceylon, Sumatra, Java, and many other Asiatic countries. But the orthodox Hindus regard the Jains as agnostics and the Buddhists as atheists; because the Jains neither accept nor deny soul or God; while the modern Buddhists in India do not believe in the existence of One Supreme Being, or in the existence of the individual soul as an eternal entity, neither do they honor the revealed word of the Vedas. For this reason they are classed by the orthodox Hindus as atheists, although Buddha himself is recognized as one of the incarnations of Vishnu. Every Hindu believes that Buddha came to help mankind, and ranks him with Râma, Krishna, and other Avatâras.

There are still other heterodox Hindus who are known as Brâhmos and Arya-Somâjis, and who may be compared to the Unitarians in this country. They reject all symbols and images, but worship One God who is personal and without form.

Thus I have given you a brief outline of the existing phases of the dualistic and qualified non-dualistic branches of the one Religion. But there is still another which is the monistic phase of the same religion. It is based upon the fundamental principle of unity in variety. It teaches that there is one existence, one reality, one truth, one substance, in the whole universe. All the distinctions and differentiations which we perceive with our senses are phenomenal, therefore transitory and unreal. This One Substance is called by various names. In the Vedas we find the first mention of this universal and eternal law of unity in variety. In the Rig Veda, which is the oldest Scripture of the world, we read: "That which exists is One; men call it by various names." Men worship it in different forms, under different names. The same Substance, the Absolute Eternal Being, manifests itself as Brahmâ the Creator, Vishnu the Preserver, Rudra the Destroyer, and Shakti the Divine Mother. The same Eternal Being is worshipped as Allah by the Mahometans, Father in Heaven and Christ by the Christians, Buddha by the Buddhists, Jina by the Jains, Ahura Mazda by the Zoroastrians, Ti-Tien by the Chinese, and Shiva, Divine Mother, or Brahman, by the Hindus. The substance is one, although the names may vary. As the one substance water is called in different languages by different names, such as aqua, wasser, eau, agua, pâni, vâri, jalam, etc., so the One Infinite Absolute Being is worshipped under different names in different countries. This phase of religion unifies all sects and creeds; and, putting each in the place where it belongs, it builds up the universal religion, which is not confined by any particular book or Scripture, but embraces all the Scriptures of the world. Its principal teaching is that the individual souls are not born in sin and iniquity, nor have they inherited as a birthright the sins of some fallen man who was tempted by an evil spirit called Satan. On the contrary, it tells us that all men and women, irrespective of their color, creed, or religious beliefs, are children of Immortal Bliss, sons of immortality; that each individual soul is immortal by its birthright, will attain to immortality, and continue to remain immortal forever. For if the soul were not immortal by nature, it could not be made so by any being, however powerful. Each soul is a storehouse of infinite potentialities and possesses infinite possibilities. It was not created out of nothing, nor by the will of some creator; but it is eternal, beginningless and endless. That is the teaching; and it declares that we are not helpless victims of our parents' sins, but that our present condition is the resultant of our past deeds, and that our future state will be the result of our present actions. Parents do not create the souls of their children; they are but the channels, the instruments through which the individual souls incarnate or manifest themselves on the physical plane. This is popularly known as the doctrine of Reincarnation, which means the remanifestation on this earth of the individual soul, or the germ of life, according to its desires and tendencies, which will determine the conditions of its existence. The Hindus accept the law of Karma and do not believe that God creates one man to enjoy and another to suffer, nor do they maintain that He punishes the wicked and rewards the virtuous. Punishment and reward are but the reactions of our own actions. Each individual soul reaps the fruits of its own acts, either here or in some other existence.

This universal religion may be called the

"Science of the Soul." As modern science does not deal with dogmas and does not insist upon belief in the authority of any person or book, but depends entirely upon correct observation and experience of the facts of nature to discover the laws which govern the phenomena of the universe, so the monistic religion does not deal with dogmas and creeds, but explains through logic and reason the spiritual nature of man or the true nature of the soul. It describes the origin, growth, and process of its gradual evolution from the minutest germ of life up to the highest spiritual man, as Christ or Buddha or Râmakrishna; for it claims that all souls will become perfect in the course of evolution. Each individual soul, however imperfect it may be at present, is bound in the end to attain perfection and become divine. It teaches that the human soul in the progress of spiritual evolution passes step by step from dualism or monotheism to qualified non-dualism, and ultimately reaches the spiritual height of absolute non-dualism or monism. So long as a soul is on the plane of duality, or of monotheism, it believes in a God who dwells outside of nature, who is extra-cosmic, who, as the Creator of the universe, creates something out of nothing, and who is far, far away from us. We cannot reach Him—He is too high, too great, too distant. He is the Master and we are His servants; we must worship Him in that relation. But when we approach nearer to the Infinite Being, we gradually begin to see that He is not so far from us, that He is immanent and resident in nature. He is near us; why should we consider Him as beyond, far out of our reach? Then we come to that phase which is called qualified non-dualistic. In this we realize that God is one stupendous whole and we are but parts; each individual soul is a part of the Infinite Being. But when the soul rises still higher, it transcends all relativity and plunges into the realm of the Absolute. There, forgetting all names and forms, it reaches absolute oneness with Divinity, and then it declares: "I and my Father are one." In that state the soul becomes perfected; all the divine qualities and divine powers begin to flow through it, and it is transfigured into

Divine Glory. Then it becomes Christ-like; it reaches that state which is represented by the word "Christ."

The word "Christ", according to the universal religion, means a state of spiritual perfection, of spiritual realization or attainment of oneness with the Supreme Being. Whosoever reaches that state becomes Christ. And this universal religion teaches that each individual soul is a potential Christ, is potentially divine, and that potentiality will become actual when the soul awakens to the consciousness of its divine glory. When, transcending all bondage, all laws of the relative, phenomenal world, it comes face to face with the Absolute, it reaches the height of monistic religion, then it will be Christ, then it will be Buddha, "the Enlightened One"—or he who has attained to spiritual enlightenment. According to this religion, when Jesus attained to that state, He became Christ; when Buddha attained to that state, He was held by the world as the Saviour of mankind, as the Redeemer. This universal religion brings great comfort and consolation to us, because it assures us that we are not going to eternal perdition; for it does not believe in hell-fire or eternal damnation. It teaches that men commit mistakes, and those mistakes will bring their results through the law of cause and sequence, of action and reaction, but they will not last throughout eternity. Death, therefore, cannot frighten the followers of this religion.

Although this universal religion is founded upon the teachings of the Vedas and is as old as the Vedas, yet it has been forgotten again and again, and again and again it has been revived and preached by the great Saviours and spiritual leaders who have flourished in India from time to time. Krishna preached it 1400 years before Christ; after the decline of Buddhism it was preached again by Sankârâcharya in the eighth century after Christ; and lastly it was preached by Bhagavân Sri Râmakrishna, who lived in the latter part of the nineteenth century and who is regarded by thousands and thousands of educated Hindus as the latest Incarnation of Divinity. He is recognized as the prime-mover in the great religious upheaval which has begun in India. The tidal wave of this universal religion, rising from Râmakrishna as its centre, has inundated the whole spiritual field of India and is rapidly spreading all over the world, creating a revolution in the world's religious thought, which will surely produce wonderful results in time to come.

III.

THE SOCIAL STATUS OF THE INDIAN PEOPLE: THEIR SYSTEM OF CASTE.

IN the last lecture we saw how the Indo-Aryans hold the loftiest ideal of absolute freedom in their religious belief. From time immemorial they have shown perfect toleration toward the followers of every faith, and no religious persecution has been recorded in the whole history of India. Even atheists and agnostics have been allowed to live unmolested. Although the Mahometans and the Christians hate the Hindus, still the Hindus do not persecute them, but live in absolute peace and harmony with them. India is indeed the home of universal tolerance and religious freedom. In their social life, on the contrary, the Hindus are more restricted than any other nation of the world. Their society is different from that of Europe or America; its laws are more rigid and binding. They will not associate or intermarry with the Mahometans or Christians, not however because of their religious beliefs, but on account of their social ideals.

The Hindu people are extremely conservative in their manners and customs, perhaps more so than the Chinese or Japanese; and this conservatism has been the outcome of long-standing foreign rule and of continuous inroads and invasions by foreign nations. We ought not to forget that India was first invaded by the Greeks, then by the Scythians, and afterward by Mongolians, Tartars, Mahometans, and lastly by the Portuguese, the Dutch, and other Christians. These powerful nations fell upon India like avalanches, devastating the land of its wealth and prosperity and destroying the glorious monuments of the Indo-Aryans. They came not to help the Hindus, but to plunder their country and rob them of their valuable possessions. What nation could withstand such successive invasions and survive such repeated disasters without possessing a tremendous power of conservatism? The Egyptians, Persians, and other nations which were unable to conserve themselves in time of need have been swept out of existence. This power of conservatism which has been so marvellously displayed by the Hindu people is indeed a great lesson to the civilized world. It has kept the nation alive, and has protected the Aryan blood and Aryan literature by creating impregnable social barriers which the destructive forces of successive invaders have never been able to break through.

No foreign power can demolish the social structure of the Hindus. It has stood for ages firm like the gigantic peaks of the Himalayas, defying the strength of all hostile forces, because its foundation was laid—not upon the quick-sand of commercialism, not upon the quagmire of greed for territorial possessions, but upon the solid rock of the moral and spiritual laws which eternally govern earthly existence. The ancient founders of Hindu society were not like the robber-barons or ambitious political leaders of mediæval Europe; but they were sages and *Seers of Truth*, who sacrificed their personal interest, their ambition and desire for power and position upon the altar of disinterested love for humanity.

The Hindus of modern times trace their descent from these great sages, saints, and Rishis of pre-historic ages, and consider themselves blessed on account of such exalted lineage. They glory in the names of their forefathers, and feel an unconquerable pride because of the purity, unselfishness, spirituality, and God-consciousness of their holy ancestors. This noble pride has prevented the members of different communities from holding free intercourse and from intermarrying with foreigners and invading nations, and has thus kept the Aryan blood pure and unadulterated. If they had not possessed that tremendous national pride and had mixed freely with all people by whom they were overrun, we should not find in India to-day the full-blooded descendants of the pure Aryan family.

Hindu society is divided into hundreds of communities; each community consists of several clans and each clan has its own peculiar customs and rules. These clans, again, are made up of numerous families, "Kula", and the members of these families are the individual units. The members of the family are governed by the "Kula-Dharma" or family customs, the families must obey the clan family customs, and the clan families must be governed by the rules of the community. The members of the family enjoy absolute freedom in everything that is approved of by the other families of the same clan. If the common opinion of the majority of the families of one clan be against any act of violation of its long-standing custom, then it should not be performed. If any one dares to violate such custom, then he forfeits all the privileges which he may have in his family life in the community. He will be deprived of social intercourse and relationship with the clan family and of the protection of the community.

This clan family is called in Sanskrit "Gotra". There is no English word by which I can translate this term, the literal meaning of "Gotra" being "lineage", that is, the descendants of common ancestors. Originally there were about twenty-four Rishis who were Gotra-makers or makers of clans. They were all sages and Seers of Truth, who lived in the Vedic period and were inspired. The hymns of the Vedas and other holy Scriptures in India came through them, and they were leaders as well as clan-makers. We all trace our descent from these great Rishis.

Again, the community of many clans is called in Sanskrit "Jâti", Greek "Genus", Roman "Gens", or the patriarchal family in the largest sense of the term. Each community consists of many clans, which live together, obeying the laws of the community. The rules of propriety and impropriety, marriage ceremonies and funeral rites, rituals and ceremonies, amusements and occupations, professions and industries, nay, all the details of social life must be in perfect harmony with the laws and customs which have been handed down through generations to the existing communities. These social laws are called "Jâti-Dharma", or the duties of a Jâti or community. Each clan family, from the lowest Pariah to the highest Brâhmin, is guided and governed by the Jâti-Dharma. No position, profession, or industry can be accepted by any member of a community if the community as a body disapproves of it. If any member wishes to fulfil a desire, he must first consider whether it is in perfect harmony with the customs of the family (Kula-Dharma), then with the duties of the clan family (Gotra-Dharma), and lastly with the laws of the community (Jâti-Dharma); and, after establishing harmony with all these, he can do what he pleases. In case of difference of opinion, whatever the community decides for the family and the individual they must implicitly obey. The leaders of the community are the final authorities. The individual sacrifices his freedom for the sake of the family, the interest of the family is merged into that of the clan, and the clan sacrifices its interest for the community.

This is a peculiar system of government, but it has existed in India for many centuries. A Hindu from the time of his birth up to his last moment lives a life which may be called a life of self-sacrifice. Whether a man or a woman, his or her ideal is not to think of himself or herself, not to seek his or her own comfort, not to enjoy selfish pleasures, but to live for the good, first, of the family, then of the clan, then of the community. Such is the custom in India. Of course this government by community we find in almost every country in some form and to some extent, but nowhere is it so strict and so perfectly organized as in India.

The communities, again, have no social rank or grade among themselves. All communities are equally great and all clans are equally good. Each community is like a small social republic in itself. The rules and customs of one community do not interfere with those of another, and in this respect every community enjoys absolute freedom as a body, but the individuals in it cannot enjoy this freedom. They must obey the laws of their community; and if they violate any existing custom they must go through certain penances and austerities. Otherwise they will be excommunicated, and excommunication is the worst punishment that can be given to a Hindu. He will not be invited by other members of the same community, neither will his invitation be accepted by them. At the time of birth, death, or wedding he will be left alone and absolutely friendless in the world. No other community will take him. Nor can he join another clan, because his birthright prevents him. Such is the rigidity and power of the communal form of social government among the Hindus.

Outsiders and foreigners do not understand this government, because they do not belong to any community, and those who do not belong to a community cannot know anything of it. These are unwritten laws. You will not find them in books; but the unwritten laws are more binding than the written laws. Strangers who go to India cannot see the reason why the members of different communities under the name of Brâhmin, Kshatriya, or any other caste do not intermarry or have free social intercourse with one another. There are, for instance, Brâhmins all over India; but a Brâhmin of Bombay will not intermarry with the Brâhmins of Calcutta, or Madras, or the Punjab. Why? Because although they are all Brâhmins, they do not belong to the same community. Again, all the Brâhmins of the Province of Bengal do not intermarry or mix freely or eat together, because they are members of different communities. The descendants of different clans (Gotra) belonging to the same community, however, will intermarry and have free social intercourse.

The tendency of each community is to preserve the clan family intact and to keep the Aryan blood of the individuals in it as pure as possible, and also to make its members live on the highest moral and spiritual plane. The community approves of everything that is truly ethical and uplifting and rejects that which debases the moral and spiritual conduct of the family or individual. Being thus protected by the laws and customs of the community, individual members grow up, rear their children, live in joint families, fulfil their social or rather communal duties, enjoy pleasures and amusements, and serve the community by performing such acts as will help other families and members of the same community. If there be a millionaire, for example, his duty is to help first his own family, then all the families of his own clan, then other families of the same community. He can then extend his charitable and philanthropic works to the members of other communities or do anything for the good of the public in general. Each community is like one family and tremendous unity exists among its members. For this reason, there never was any need in India of such philanthropic organizations and asylums as you have in Europe and America. Orphanages, poorhouses, and charitable institutions were not necessary, because the community took care of its own poor and its own orphans. You put the poorer classes in asylums; but we take them into our homes, feed them, and clothe them. That is our duty, because they are our brothers. No grander system was ever established in the world.

Hindu leaders of society, after trying various methods, discovered that this form of social government was the best suited for the Hindu people. Their idea was that if all the existing communities into which the whole Hindu population is divided enforced these moral and spiritual laws among the members of the different families then the whole nation would be moral and spiritual; just as the whole street will be clean if every one keeps the front of his house clean. Thus they started from these individual units and built up a system upon natural laws, making one family of the whole nation.

But these communities at present are not perfect. They have now become fixed entities; their laws, rules, and ideals have lost their flexible nature and have become so rigid and binding that they cannot be changed, for they are considered to represent the highest and best ideals. But the individual living within the limits of the community may change his ideas and adopt new ones, better suited to immediate conditions, which will put him at variance with the communal life and alienate him from his clan family. Herein lies one of the serious defects of the present system. This government by community, however, is more effective and beneficial than the church government such as we find in this country. Why? Because social questions must be kept separate from religion; otherwise there will be religious dissension and persecution. And this is the secret of religious toleration in India. Religion is never interfered with on account of social affairs. As I explained in my last lecture, the Hindus are absolutely free to choose any form of worship they like, but that has nothing to do with their social status. The government by community, however imperfect it may be, has at least this advantage,—that it gives freedom in religion and confers upon all the members of these communities equal rights, equal privileges, and equal opportunities. Both men and women are allowed the same right to discuss and vote upon any disputed question.

Each community has its aristocracy, middle classes, and lower classes. The lower and middle classes aspire to rise to the higher ranks of the community and expect favor, help, and support from the superior classes. A man may possess enormous wealth in the community, but he can never change his birthright. Neither will he change his clan (Gotra) or community (Jâti).

No other clan will accept him as a member, no other community will give him better privileges or protection. The social status of a Hindu depends upon the rights which he or she has acquired by birth in the family, clan, and community. There was, for example, a community of fishermen. A lady in that community inherited a large estate. In India the women hold property, manage their own estates, and in such matters have great freedom. Now this lady had unusual power and ability and she managed her property most admirably. She built temples, performed other charitable and philanthropic works, and did incalculable good by her example to all the members of the families and clans of the same community. She was considered to be like the queen of that community. All of its members honored and respected her as the jewel of their society, as did the communities of Brâhmins and other castes; but she never thought of changing her clan or of rejecting the laws and customs of her own community.

These communities, again, are subdivisions of larger classes, which are known in English as "castes." The word "caste" has become most mischievous and misleading, and the less we use it the better we shall be able to understand the social conditions of the people of ancient and modern India. The term "caste" is the anglicized form of the Portuguese word "casta", which means "breed" or "stock." It was first applied by the rough Portuguese sailors of the sixteenth century to certain divisions of the Hindu society. It was originally used in the sense of pure, unmixed breed, but in Sanskrit there is no equivalent of such a word as caste. In the writings of the Hindus, from the Vedas down to the Laws of Manu and the Purânas, we do not find any word which has the same meaning as is conveyed by the term caste, and in India to ask a Hindu what is meant by caste would be like asking an American what caste means in America. The Sanskrit word which has been translated (or mistranslated) by caste is "Varna" (color), which implied some ethnological distinction of complexion as separating the dominant from the inferior classes, the Aryans from the non-Aryan aboriginal tribes of ancient India. Mr. R. C. Dutt says: "The very word 'Varna', which in later Sanskrit indicates caste, is used in the Rig Veda to distinguish the Aryans and the non-Aryans, and nowhere indicates separate sections in the Aryan community." * This distinction of color, however, gradually gave rise to separate divisions in the Aryan community itself; as in the Bhagavad Gita we read: "The Lord has divided the whole human race into four classes, according to their color, qualifications, qualities, and works." † The four original colors of different races were white, red, yellow, and black; and the intermixture of these four original colors has produced all the various race divisions of the world. Among the Aryans those who were white in color were called Brâhmins; the red, Kshatriyas; the yellow, Vaishyas; and the black, Sudras. Again the different qualities and works of these four classes are thus described: "The duties of Brâhmins, Kshatriyas, Vaishyas, as also of Sudras, are divided in accordance with

* Civilization in Ancient India, Vol. I, p. 65.

† Chapter IV, verse 13.

their nature-born qualities. Peace, self-restraint, austerities, purity, forgiveness, and uprightness, knowledge, direct intuition, and faith in God are the natural qualities of the Brâhmin. Of the Kshatriyas, bravery, energy, fortitude, dexterity, fleeing not in battle, gift and lordliness are the nature-born qualities. Agriculture, protection of cows, merchandise, and various industries are the nature-born duties of the Vaishyas. Conscientiousness in menial service is the nature-born duty of the Sudras. A man attains perfection by performing those duties which he is able to do." * Here you see a man's caste was determined not only by his color but also by his natural qualifications. That was the original idea behind all caste distinctions among the Hindus. It is quite different from the explanation given by foreigners and missionaries.

The Brâhmins were naturally qualified to fulfil certain duties, and they discharged them faithfully and perfectly. Propelled by a nature-born tendency they devoted themselves to the study of the various branches of science and phi-

* Bhagavad Gita, Chapter XVIII, verses 41–45.

losophy, as well as the Vedic Scriptures, and performed the religious rites and ceremonies of all classes of people and other priestly duties. The Kshatriyas were those who became warriors, soldiers, commanders, and rulers of the country. The trades, industries, and agriculture were managed by the Vaishyas; while the Sudras were those who were qualified to do only the menial and domestic service in the household life of the other three classes. Thus there arose a complete system of division of labor. To every man his place, work, rank, and remuneration were assigned.

This division was made perhaps during the Vedic period, or perhaps earlier; but we find it given in the Vedas. When the Aryans first invaded India from Central Asia they were highly civilized. They knew agriculture, and had wonderful social and political organizations. And when a division of labor became necessary, they divided themselves into different classes in accordance with their natural tendencies. But at first these divisions were flexible and interchangeable. The social distinctions were not iron-bound; neither were the occupations and professions hereditary. We read in the Vedas and other ancient writings of the Hindus that the Brâhmins could intermarry with the Kshatriyas, Vaishyas, and Sudras. They could also become warriors if they were so qualified; while the Kshatriyas often became the teachers of the Brâhmins; in fact, most of the philosophical and spiritual ideals which we have to-day were first given by the Kshatriyas, and not by the Brâhmins. The members of these classes mixed freely, and whenever any one had the qualifications of a Brâhmin or a Kshatriya he was called Brâhmin or Kshatriya. There were many Kshatriyas who were afterward called Brâhmins on account of their spiritual wisdom and greatness. You will notice that almost all the incarnations of Divinity in India were Kshatriyas, and very few were Brâhmins. Another theory about the origin of caste is given in the Mahâbhârata. In the Shanti Parva (chs. 188–189) we read:

"A sage Bharadvâja asks another sage Bhrigu:

"If color is the principle of differentiation of caste in the fourfold caste system, then there is indeed seen the confusion of color among all castes;

"'Desire, anger, fear, avarice, grief, anxiety, hunger, and weariness sway all of us, how then is the division of caste?

"'Innumerable are the species of moving and unmoving beings; of these various classes, whence the determination of castes?'

"Bhrigu replied:

"'There is no distinction of castes. The whole world being created by Brahmâ in the beginning consisted of Brâhmins only. By actions it underwent (the distinctions of) caste.

"'Those twice-born men or Brâhmins, who were fond of the enjoyment of desires, fierce, passionate, and daring in (the pursuit of) desired objects, who had abandoned their own duties, men of ruddy complexion,—these attained the rank of Kshatriyas.

"'Those twice-born men or Brâhmins, who had taken to the profession of tending cattle, who were yellow in color, lived by agriculture, and abode not by their own duties,—these attained the rank of Vaishyas.

"Those twice-born men or Brâhmins, who were fond of killing and telling falsehoods, covetous, who lived by all (kinds of) occupations, dark in color, and who abandoned all cleanliness,—these attained the rank of Sudras.

"Separated by these actions, the twice-born have undergone differentiation into castes."

These four main divisions of the Indo-Aryans of the Vedic period, according to their *Varna* (color) and occupations gradually lost their flexible nature and became a system of hereditary caste as early as six centuries before Christ, when Buddha arose as a great reformer against the separation and distinction of castes. He gave a death-blow to priestly power and equalized all classes of people by breaking down the barriers of this artificial hereditary caste division. Under this system if a Brâhmin was a priest, his son must be a priest also; while the son of a Kshatriya (soldier) must be a soldier. This was of course started at first with the idea of perfecting the different lines of work, and the ancient thinkers and social leaders understood the laws of heredity so thoroughly that they tried to develop the best qualities through hereditary transmission. Buddha, however, strove to bring the whole social system into its original simple form and make it as flexible as it was at the outset. He would not recognize a Brâhmin because he was born a Brâhmin, but he distinguished all people according to their merits and qualifications. Any one who possessed the beautiful qualities of peace, self-restraint, self-control, righteousness, devotion, love for humanity, and divine wisdom, was called by him a Brâhmin; * and during the period of nearly a thousand years, while Buddhism reigned over India, people of different classes forgot their hereditary caste distinctions and enjoyed social and political freedom.

About 600 A.D., however, Buddhism declined, corruptions crept in, and the orthodox Brâhmins, regaining their power, reëstablished the original social organization in accordance with the hereditary system of class divisions. Then later the Mahometans came, and for six hundred years tried in vain to destroy the social structure of

* *Vide* Dhammapada, Chapter XXVI.

the Hindus. Whoever favored the Mahometan ideals was ostracized and excommunicated by the Hindus. Thus Hindu society lost many of its most brilliant men and women. Those who intermarried or associated freely with the Mahometans were deprived of all social rights in their community, and under no circumstances could be taken back by the Hindus. Such was the tyranny and abuse of power exercised by the fanatical descendants of the great Aryan Rishis and sages of ancient India. The Brâhmins and social leaders of the middle ages were short-sighted and superstitious; they had love of power, they wished to rule over the people and keep them under their control. To-day India would be one of the mightiest nations in the world if these short-sighted orthodox social leaders had not pursued a policy of seclusion and isolation, which resulted in absolute disunion among the members of the different classes of the Hindus. England could not have held her dominant sword over the heads of three hundred millions of people in India if there had been unity among the isolated communities and clans of the four divisions. Well has it been said by Sir Monier Monier Williams: "And certainly the antagonism of these caste associations and trade leagues has helped us to govern the country by making political combinations impracticable." *

But now the conditions are changing. India of to-day is different from what she was fifty years ago. Education and intellectual progress are opening the eyes of the nation. The cry for social reform is to be heard in every corner of this vast country. People are beginning to see the defects of the existing social organism. The educated classes are now convinced that if the present conditions are allowed to continue the absolute disintegration and complete annihilation of the national life will be the inevitable result. Thinking people are no longer satisfied with the seclusion and isolation of the different communities by iron barriers of superstition. They wish to unify all communities into one homogeneous whole, to make every member feel that he is a part and parcel, not merely of a family, clan, or community, not merely a part

* Brâhminism and Hinduism, p. 474.

of a section of the Hindu nation which is limited by color or caste, but a most important part of the Indo-Aryan nation as a whole. The solidarity of all classes and all communities is the aim of the social reformers. The work has begun, but it will take a long time to make this reform effective and universal.

To-day the integrity of the social organization is weakened; social chaos and anarchy have prevailed. Fifty years ago every one was proud of his noble birth, but with the hard competition and extreme poverty of the masses, brought about by an alien government, the question of bread and butter has absorbed the whole attention of the people. The people to-day are very poor. They need food and clothes and a shelter over their heads. They have no means to support their families. Their present social status depends upon wealth. A high-class Brâhmin, disregarding the ancient tradition and custom of his caste, will now perform the most menial tasks, like cooking in a private house or working as a servant. To-day the question is how to live. A Brâhmin again will bow down to a Sudra of the lowest class if the latter happens to be rich. Twenty years ago the brother looked upon his elder as his superior, but now he considers him merely as a good companion. The rigors of the social organization, which formerly ensured obedience to authority have been loosened, and every one now feels that he is at liberty to go his own way.

The Hindus are passing through a transition period. Social progress is at present checked by the vigorous efforts of an unsympathetic, greedy, selfish, and despotic foreign government, whose heartless officials are sucking the life-blood of the Hindu nation. All the trade guilds and industrial leagues which exercised such tremendous power in the social life of the Hindus have no longer voice or authority in the community. English merchants, protected by the British government, have taken possession of the market, have driven out the native manufacturers, have destroyed the trade and commerce of the country, and have thus ruined millions of people. If you go to India to-day, you will find thousands and thousands, perhaps millions and millions, who have no occupation. No industry is encouraged. People are driven to live upon agriculture. The English government wanted to make India an agricultural country and she has succeeded in doing so. The laboring classes in consequence are obliged to live and support their family on from two to five cents a day. What social progress can we expect to see under such destructive power vigorously exercised by the so-called monarch of European civilization? Christian missionaries, blinded by their fanatical zeal to Christianize India, do not see the faults and the demoralizing influence of the present system of despotic government which is ruining the country, but they trace the origin of all social evils to the religion of the Hindus. Directly or indirectly their efforts are to destroy the Hindu social structure, but have they any better system to give in return? We see that the present social government in Europe and in this country is not perfect. It is not even as perfect as the corrupted caste system which exists in India! These Christian missionaries do not realize that the majority of the Christian converts in India repent as long as they live for the great mistake they have committed in alienating themselves from the Hindu society. Have they any social standing even among the Christians themselves? Are the negroes of America on an equal footing with the white Christians? No. First let the Christians root out from their hearts the prejudice against race and color. Have they succeeded in doing that? How then can they solve the tremendous social problem which faces the Hindu people? India needs social reconstruction, but will they find that through Christianity? No, Christianity cannot help them, because the Christians know how to destroy, but they do not know how to build—especially in India. They may give their church government, which would be worse in a country like India. The people have suffered enough from priestcraft; they do not want any more of it.

India needs social reorganization and social regeneration. The Christians, like the Mahometans, have poured their ideals into the sea of Hindu society and have created waves of radical reform. To-day the waters of that social sea are being constantly stirred by the anglicized and half-Europeanized reformers of the present generation. Now the time has come for the Hindu leaders of society to stand on a broader and more universal platform and reconstruct their system, accepting whatever is good and noble among Western nations and adding it to their own lofty ideals. They will have to make their social organization more flexible than it has ever been. That reconstruction must be based upon the broadest and most universal ideals of the Hindu nation, tempered by the need of occidental aggressiveness and commercialism. The remedy has already been discovered in the all-embracing and unifying system of Vedanta, which, proclaiming the divine right of all humanity irrespective of caste, creed, or color, and teaching that all are children of God, whether Christians or Hindus, Pariahs or Brâhmins, will once more purify the social conditions, remove the evils of the caste system, uplift the individuals, bring solidarity among the members of different communities, and make the Hindu nation stand once more as a great civilizing power among the civilized nations of the world.

IV.

POLITICAL INSTITUTIONS OF INDIA.

THOSE who have studied the history of the civilization of ancient India are well acquainted with the fact that the Hindus were highly civilized at least five thousand years ago. The earliest records of Hindu civilization are to be found in the Rig Veda, the oldest Scriptures of the world, and in other writings of the Vedic period. From these sources we learn, as was shown in the last lecture, that the Indo-Aryans of those prehistoric times organized their society into four general classes: Brâhmins, Kshatriyas, Vaishyas, and Sudras, according to their color, qualifications, and professions. The Brâhmins were entrusted with literary and priestly duties; while the Kshatriyas were those who devoted their energy to protect the country against invaders, to govern the land, and to look after the welfare and safety of all the other classes. Industry, trade, commerce, agriculture, and the various duties of a commercial life were undertaken by those who were known as the Vaishyas or the merchant class; and the Sudras belonged to the serving class.

The Vedic writings also tell us that the Indo-Aryans of those days cultivated the land with ploughs, used oxen and horses in the field, understood irrigation by means of canals, and knew the use of wells and reservoirs for drinking as well as for irrigation. Various kinds of industry, trade, and commerce, as also the existence of current money—like pieces of gold of a certain fixed value, for use in buying and selling are mentioned in the Rig Veda. The Indo-Aryans, we read, furthermore, were continually engaged in fighting against the non-Aryan aboriginal tribes who were the original inhabitants of India, and remnants of whom are still to be found in some parts among the hill tribes, just as you find to-day some of the original inhabitants of America in certain parts of this country. In these battles with hostile tribes "the (Aryan) warriors used not only armour and helmets, but also protecting armour for the shoulder, probably shields. They used javelins and battle-axes, and sharp-edged swords, besides bows and arrows. All the weapons of war known elsewhere in ancient times were known in India four thousand years ago. Drums assembled men in battle, banners led them on in compact masses, and the use of war horses and chariots was well known. Tame elephants were in use too." *

The Rig Veda contains numerous allusions which show that the use of iron, gold, and of other metals was well known to the Hindus. Armors worn in war are mentioned in Book I, 140, 10; in II, 39, 4; in IV, 53, 2, as in various other places; while the javelin, in Sanskrit *Rishti*, and the battle-axe, *Bashi* in Sanskrit, are mentioned in the Rig Veda, V, 52, 6, and 57, 2. Three thousand mailed warriors are spoken of in the same Veda, VI, 27, 6; and sharp-edged swords are described in VI, 47, 10. That the arrowheads were made of iron is shown in

* "Civilization in Ancient India," Vol. I, p. 58.

Book VI, 75, 15: "We extol the arrow which is poisoned whose face is iron," and in the next book (83, 1) we read: "When the battle is nigh and the warrior marches in his armour, he appears like the cloud."

It was by ceaseless fighting that the ancient Indo-Aryans protected themselves in their newly-conquered country, extended the limits of cultivation, and built new towns and villages. This interminable warring and fighting forced the conquering Aryan tribes to organize their political and military institutions. Thus the political institutions of the Hindus are as old as their civilization. They divided the country into various kingdoms, principalities, and chiefships, each enjoying perfect autonomy. At the head of each province or kingdom was a Hindu chief or governor, who was called a Râjah, which means "prince" or "king." These Râjahs were absolutely independent of one another. They entertained friendly relations with the Râjahs of other neighboring provinces, and sometimes they were jealous of each other. But there never was a universal sovereignty over the whole of

India, like that of the great autocrat of Russia, although there were powerful monarchs and emperors to whom other kings, chiefs, and governors of states acknowledged subordination and paid tribute. Their autonomy, however, was never sacrificed. Their alliances generally bore the character of confederacies, or federal unions, and not that of feudal baronies subject to a ruling chief; and under no circumstances were the servile duties of the feudal barons of Europe exacted from the weaker Râjahs or governors. The bond between them was of the feeblest kind, and easily broke at every favorable opportunity. In the Vedic period, there were many such emperors or Chakravartins, as they were called in Sanskrit. In the Râmâyana we read that Râma was the emperor of Ayodhyâ (modern Oudh), and his power extended all over northern and southern India as far down as Ceylon. From the Mahâbhârata, which contains the history of the Hindus who lived as early as 1400 B.C., we learn that Yudhishthira became the emperor of India after the battle of Kurukshetra. His successors, Parikshit, Janmejaya, and many others, were known as emperors. These emperors had a number of Râjahs under them, who paid allegiance and tribute to them. But their bond could break at any time for very insignificant causes.

When Alexander the Great invaded India, there was on the throne the most powerful Buddhist emperor, Chandra Gupta, whose capital was Pâtaliputra, modern Patna, on the river Ganges. His grandson was Asoka, who lived in 260 B.C. and became the most celebrated emperor of those days. He was like Constantine the Great among the Buddhists. He made Buddhism the state religion of India; he sent missionaries from Siberia to Ceylon, from China to Egypt, and made treaties with kings of foreign countries. One of the edicts of Asoka, which were written during his lifetime, says that he made treaties with five Greek kings who were his contemporaries, namely, Antiochus of Syria, Ptolemaos of Egypt, Antigonus of Macedon, Magus of Cyrene, and Alexander of Epiros; and he sent missionaries to those places, as far as Alexandria, to preach the Gospel of Buddha.

Alexander the Great, however, invaded only the northwestern corner of India, and defeated in one battle some of the hill-tribes, but afterwards, when he heard of the power and strength of Chandra Gupta, he withdrew his troops and returned to Greece. His successor, Seleucus, sent the Greek ambassador Megasthenes, who lived for several years at the court of this great emperor. From the accounts of Megasthenes, which are the most authentic historical records that we can gather from an outsider, we learn many facts about the political institutions of the Hindus as witnessed by a foreigner during the fourth century B.C. Megasthenes left a valuable record of the actual work of administration as observed by him. He says: "Those who have charge of the city are divided into six bodies of five each. The members of the first look after everything relating to the industrial arts. Those of the second attend to the entertainment of foreigners. To those they assign lodgings, and they keep watch over their modes of life by means of those persons whom they give to them for assistants. They escort them on the way when they leave the country, or, in the event of their dying, forward their property to their relatives. They take care of them when they are sick, and, if they die, bury them. The third body consists of those who inquire when and how births and deaths occur, with a view not only of levying a tax, but also in order that births and deaths among both high and low may not escape the cognizance of government. The fourth class superintends trade and commerce. Its members have charge of weights and measures, and see that the products in their season are sold by public notice. No one is allowed to deal in more than one kind of commodity unless he pays a double tax. The fifth class supervises manufactured articles, which they sell by public notice., What is new is sold separately from what is old, and there is a fine for mixing the two together. The sixth and last class consists of those who collect the tenths of the prices of the articles sold."

The military officers "also consist of six divisions, with five members to each. One division is appointed to coöperate with the admiral of the fleet; another with the superintendent of the bullock-trains which are used for transporting engines of war, food for the soldiers, provender for the cattle, and other military requisites. . . . The third division has charge of the foot-soldiers, the fourth of the horses, the fifth of the war-chariots, and the sixth of the elephants."

In addition to the military and municipal officers, there was a third class whose duty was to superintend agriculture, irrigation, forests, and the general work of administration in rural districts. "Some superintend the rivers, measure the land, as is done in Egypt, and inspect the sluices by which water is let out from the main canals into their branches, so that every one may have an equal supply of it. The same persons have charge also of the huntsmen, and are entrusted with the power of rewarding or punishing them according to their deserts. They collect the taxes, and superintend the occupations connected with land, as those of the woodcutters, the carpenters, the blacksmiths, and the miners. They construct roads, and at every ten stadia set up a pillar to show the by-roads and distances." *

The laws of war among the Hindus were more humane than among the other nations of the world, and Megasthenes mentions this fact. All these Râjahs governed their country in accordance with their laws and for the welfare of their people, and what accounts we get from Megasthenes are exactly the same as those we read in Manu, Apastamba, and other Sanskrit law-books of ancient time. Regarding the military law, or the laws of war, the Hindu lawgiver Apastamba says: "The Aryans forbid the slaughter of those who have laid down their arms, of those who beg for mercy with flying hair or joined hands, and of fugitives." (II, 5, 10, 11.) "Let him not fight with those who are in fear, intoxicated, insane or out of their minds, nor with those who have lost their armour, nor with women, infants, aged men, and Brâhmins." (Bodhayana, I, 10, 18, 11.) "The wives of slain soldiers were always provided for." (Vasishtha XIX, 20.) Megasthenes says: "For whereas among other

* MacCrindle's Translation.

nations it is usual, in the contests of war, to ravage the soil, and thus to reduce it to an uncultivated waste, among the Indians, on the contrary, by whom husbandmen are regarded as a class that is sacred and inviolable, the tillers of the soil, even when battle is raging in the neighborhood, are undisturbed by any sense of danger.... Besides, they (the warriors) never ravage an enemy's land with fire nor cut down its trees. They never use the conquered as slaves." *

The duties of the king, according to the lawgiver Manu, were "to protect his subjects, to deal impartial justice, and to punish the wrongdoer." (VII, 12, 16.) These were the three principal duties. "Drinking, gambling and licentiousness, and hunting were the most pernicious faults of the king." (VII, 50.) The private life of kings is described by Manu thus: "The king should rise in the last watch of the night, and, having performed his personal purification and devotional exercises, he should enter the hall of audience in the morning. There he

* MacCrindle's Translation.

should gratify all subjects who come to see him, and, having dismissed them, he should take counsel with his ministers in a private chamber." (VII, 145–147.) "When the consultation is over, then he is ready to take care of his physical needs, meals, and so on." But his first duty is to give an audience to his subjects and to gratify their demands. "In the afternoon, the king should review his army, inspect his fighting-men, his chariots, animals, and weapons, and then perform his twilight devotions. After this he should give audience to his secret spies and hear private reports." (VII, 221–225.) "The king was always assisted by his council of seven or eight ministers," as we read in the laws of Manu (VII, 54–63), "who were versed in sciences, skilled in the use of weapons, and descended from noble and well-tried families. Such ministers used to advise the king in matters of peace and war, revenue and religious gifts. The king also employed suitable persons for the collecting of revenue, and in mines, manufactories, and storehouses; and he employed ambassadors for carrying on negotiations with rulers." For the protection of villages and towns, separate officers were appointed. The king appointed a lord over each village, over ten villages, lords of twenty, of a hundred, and of a thousand villages; and these lords were not merely governors, but they used to check crime and protect the villages. These were the special duties of these special officers. They were like superintendents. Similarly, each town had its superintendent of all affairs, who personally inspected the work of all officials and got secret information about their behavior and private character, because the Hindu law says: "The servants of the king, who are appointed to protect the people, generally become knaves, who seize the property of others; let him protect his subjects against such men. (Manu, VII, 115–123.) From this you will see that, in ancient times, government officials used to become knaves, as they do now in a highly civilized country like America. Think of the time when this law was written,—centuries before Christ!

The income of the state from the royal demesnes was supplemented by taxes. Manu fixes an income tax of two per cent on cattle and gold. The land revenue varied from one-sixth to one-eighth or one-twelfth of the crops,* and this was much less than the land-revenue tax under British rule. Under the Hindu rule, the king was strictly prohibited from exacting excessive taxation. He was allowed to take one-sixteenth part of the price made on butter, earthen vessels and stone wares, and might exact a day's service in each month from artisans, mechanics, and other working-people; that is, one day in a month these people would give their service free. Of course, they were maintained by the king, that is, they were fed by the king at that time; and with this institution, in ancient times, they could erect wonderful buildings, palaces, and monuments for public use, which now they cannot do because the cost is so great.

All these and other laws regarding administration and taxation show that an advanced system of government prevailed in India before the beginning of the Christian era. Megasthenes,

* *Vide* Civilization in Ancient India, Vol. II, p. 102.

who lived in India in the fourth century before Christ, as also the Chinese travellers, Fa Hian, who visited India about 400 A.D., and Houen Tsang, who came to India about 630 A.D. and resided there for nearly fifteen years, spoke in the highest terms of praise of the government and administration of the Hindu Râjahs. Frequently we hear that the Hindus were so badly governed at that time that they had no peace or justice and were constantly engaged in fighting; but these witnesses of other nations, who came from other countries and lived in India, left records which speak differently. They do not cite one single instance of a people being ground down by taxes, or harassed by the arbitrary acts of kings, or ruined by famines, plagues, or internecine wars. On the contrary, they say: "The people were happy, prosperous, enjoying peace and justice. Agriculture flourished, the fine arts were cultivated." Houen Tsang, in his diary, which has been translated into English by Samuel Beal, wrote thus, describing the administration of India: "As the administration of the country is conducted on benign principles, the executive is simple. . . . The private demesnes of the crown are divided into four principal parts: the first is for carrying out the affairs of state and providing sacrificial offerings; the second is for providing subsidies for the ministers and chief officers of state; the third is for rewarding men of distinguished ability; and the fourth is for charity to religious bodies, whereby the field of merit is cultivated. In this way the taxes on the people are light, and the personal service required of them is moderate. Each one keeps his own worldly goods in peace, and all till the ground for their subsistence. Those who cultivate the royal estates pay a sixth part of the produce as tribute. The merchants who engage in commerce come and go in carrying out their transactions. The river passages and the road barriers are open on payment of a small toll. When the public works require it, labour is exacted, but paid for. The payment is in strict proportion to the work done.

"The military guard the frontiers, or go out to punish the refractory. They also mount guard at night round the palace. The soldiers are levied according to the requirements of the service; they are promised certain payments, and are publicly enrolled. The governors, ministers, magistrates, and officials have each a portion of land assigned to them for their personal support."

Houen Tsang also says that tributary kings from China sent hostages to Kanishka, the great Buddhist emperor, who reigned in Kashmir (Northwestern India) about 78 A.D., and he treated them with special favor, and set apart for their residence that portion of the country which afterwards was named Chinapati. The Chinese introduced the pear and the peach into India, "wherefore the peach is called Chinâni and the pear is called Chinarâjaputra (son of the Chinese monarch)."

Such political conditions existed in India from the time of Megasthenes down to Houen Tsang; that means from nearly the fourth century B.C. to the seventh century A. D. Besides these, the most remarkable feature of the political organization of ancient India was the village community and municipal institutions. This village community was called "Panchâyat," or committee of five. There was originally a committee of five, then afterwards it was increased to twelve. Each community formed itself into an independent little republic, which managed its own affairs and governed itself, but which was bound to the central government by the regular payment of an assessment or tax on the produce. Each district, again, was divided into territories which were governed by the village community, or "Panchâyat." Under this self-government by community, every individual member enjoyed absolute political freedom and independence. Each had full voice in the government. This government by Panchâyat is described in Manu and in other law-books of ancient India, and it has always existed among the Hindus. The people first elected their head-man, or president, who was a kind of mayor, and who was paid by a fixed proportion of land. He was the chairman of the village or town council, and used to call regular meetings. The next important officer of the community was the notary, or local attorney, who transacted the village business and kept an account of the land and produce, the rents and assessments. Then there was a Brâhmin priest, a village schoolmaster, a barber, a carpenter, a blacksmith, a cowman, a shoemaker, a potter, a washerman, a druggist, an oilman, the watchman, and the sweeper. These made up the village community. These members discussed and managed the whole affairs of the territory.

From the time of Manu, or from at least four hundred years before Christ, this form of municipal institution has existed in India, undisturbed by foreign invasions and political convulsions, internal wars, famine, plague, or earthquake. Sir Monier Monier Williams says: "And here I may observe that no circumstance in the history of India is more worthy of investigation than the antiquity and permanence of her village and municipal institutions. The importance of the study lies in the light thereby thrown on the parcelling out of rural society into autonomous institutions, like those of our own English parishes, wherever Aryan races have occupied the soil in Asia or in Europe. The Indian village or township, meaning thereby not merely a collection of houses forming a village or town, but a division of territory, perhaps three or four miles or more in extent, with its careful distribution of fixed occupations for the common good, with its intertwining and inter-dependence of individual, family, and communal interests, with its provision for political independence and autonomy, is the original type, the first germ, of all the divisions of rural and civic society in mediæval and modern Europe. It has existed almost unaltered since the description of its organization in Manu's code, two or three centuries before the Christian era. It has survived all the religious, political, and physical convulsions from which India has suffered from time immemorial. Invader after invader has ravaged the country with fire and sword, . . . but the simple, self-contained Indian township has preserved its constitution intact, its customs, precedents, and peculiar institutions, unchanged and unchangeable, amid all other changes." *

* Brâhminism and Hinduism, p. 455.

During the Mahometan rule of six hundred years, all these political institutions of the Hindus remained unaltered. They were never modified or disturbed. The Hindu villagers did not know that they were governed by the Mahometans. The throne was occupied by a Mahometan or Mogul emperor, to whom the native Râjahs and queens paid tribute, but beyond that they had no obligation; they were quite independent. Each Râjah had his own laws, his own court, and his own separate administration. The government of the country according to the Hindu system has always been continued in the native states. Even at the present time there are native states governed by Hindu Râjahs where you will still find this kind of government. The Mahometans never gained absolute control over the whole of India. Before the advent of the British rule, the administration of justice, the repression of crime, and other functions of the police, the collection of cesses and taxes, were all carried out by the government of the village community. To-day in British India this self-government of the Hindus has been destroyed by the short-sighted policy of the British autocrats, and its place has been given to a most costly system of judicial administration, unparalleled in the history of the world. They talk about English justice. Of course there is justice in English government, but it is very expensive and one-sided. Indians have justice among Indians, but if an Indian's rights are outraged by a European he cannot hope for similar justice. The poorer classes, furthermore, cannot pay for justice under any conditions; it is too expensive. The present oppression of the police and the cruelty of revenue collectors under British management have already driven the masses to the verge of absolute despair and rebellion.

Many people in this country think that England conquered India by force of arms, but history tells us that some English merchants first came to India to trade at the time when the Mahometan power was in its decline, and the Hindus were fighting against the Mahometans to throw off their yoke and reëstablish Hindu power upon the throne of Delhi. At this time of anarchy and revolution, these British traders, under the name of the East India Company, took the side of the Mahometans and gained the confidence of the last of the Mogul emperors, who was then merely a titular sovereign. He had lost all power; nobody obeyed him. As a return for what he had received from the East India Company and as a favor to Lord Clive, this last of the Mogul emperors, in 1765, gave a charter making the East India Company of British traders the Dewan, or administrators, of Bengal. Though the Great Mogul had no real power to do such a thing, still, as long as he was the titular sovereign of India, his charter gave the East India Company a legal status in the country. The officers of the Company held that charter in their hands wherever they went. Lord Clive himself, in his letter to the Court of Directors from Calcutta dated September 30, 1765, writes: "The assistance which the Great Moghal had received from our arms and treasury made him readily bestow this grant upon the Company." "I mean the *Dewanee*, which is the superintendency of all the lands and the collection of all the revenues of the provinces of Bengal, Behar, and Orissa." These three provinces first came into the hands of the East India Company, and at that period the revenue from them was enormous. Lord Clive writes again: "Your revenues, by means of this acquisition, will, as near as I can judge, not fall far short, for the ensuing year, of 250 lacks of Sicca Rupees,* including your former possession of Burdwan, etc. Hereafter they will at least amount to twenty or thirty lacks more. Your civil and military expenses in time of peace can never exceed sixty lacks of Rupees; the Nabob's allowances are already reduced to forty-two lacks, and the tribute to the king (the Great Moghal) at twenty-six; so that there will be remaining a clear gain to the Company of 122 lacks of Sicca Rupees, or £1,650,900 sterling." † "An annual remittance of over a million and a half sterling was to be made from a subject country to the shareholders (of the East India Company) in Engliand." ‡

* Three rupees make one dollar; a lack was 100,000 rupees.

† House of Commons Third Report, 1773, Appendix, pp. 391–398.

‡ Economic History of British India, p. 39.

This was the beginning of British empire in India. That annual remittance has now increased and swelled to nearly thirty million pounds sterling. "The scheme of administration introduced by Clive was a sort of dual government. The collection of revenues was still made for the (Mahometan) Nawab's exchequer; justice was still administered by the Nawab's officers; and all transactions were covered by the mask of the Nawab's authority. But the East India Company, the real masters of the country derived all the profits; and the Company's servants practised unbounded tyranny for their own gain, overawing the Nawab's servants, and converting his tribunals of justice into instruments for the prosecution of their own purposes.* It is a long story; time will not permit me to describe the harrowing tales of the foul and treacherous methods which were adopted by the unworthy representatives of the English people, under the name of the East India Company, to secure for their motherland a market-place for her trade and commerce, and to bring benefit and prosperity

* Economic History of British India, p. 42.

to the British nation, which was at that time the poorest nation in Europe. Those who have read the impeachment of Warren Hastings by Burke, as also impartial students of the history of the East India Company, are already acquainted with the brutal policy of the Company, which has ruined the most prosperous country of India. Zemindars were dispossessed of their hereditary rights, their lands were let to the highest bidder by public auction, trade and manufacture were destroyed by monopoly and coercion, prohibitive duties were charged on manufactured articles, etc.

Terrible famines began for the first time with the British rule in India. In 1770 there was a terrible famine in the district of Purneah, in Bengal, in which above one-third of the population died of starvation; but the revenue from land-tax was exacted with such tyranny and oppression that even during that famine it was larger than in previous years. On the 9th of May, 1770, the Calcutta Council wrote to the Court of Directors: "The famine which has ensued, the mortality, the beggary, exceed all description.

Above one-third of the inhabitants have perished in the once plentiful province of Purneah, and in other parts the misery is equal." On the 12th of February, 1771, they wrote: "Notwithstanding the great severity of the late famine, and the great reduction of the people thereby, some increase has been made in the settlements (of taxes) both of the Bengal and the Behar provinces for the present year." * Mr. Dutt says in his Economic History of India: "Famines in India are directly due to a deficiency in the annual rainfall; but the intensity of such famines and the loss of lives caused by them are largely due to the chronic poverty of the people. If the people were generally in a prosperous condition, they could make up for local failure of crops by purchases from neighboring provinces, and there would be no loss of life. But when the people are absolutely resourceless, they cannot buy from surrounding tracts, and they perish in hundreds of thousands, or in millions, whenever there is a local failure of crops." †

* Extracts from India Office Records quoted in Hunter's "Annals of Rural Bengal," 1868, pp. 21, 399.

† P. 51.

The reports of the Indian Famine Commissions of 1880 and 1898 show that between 1860 and 1900, that is, within forty years, there were ten widespread famines in India. In 1860 a famine broke out in Northern India and the loss of life was estimated at 200,000, but was probably much larger; in 1866 a famine in Orissa carried off one-third of the population, or about a million people; in 1869 there was another famine in Northern India, during which at least 1,200,000 people died; in 1874 Bengal was visited by famine, but the land-tax in this province is light and is *permanently settled*; the people are therefore comparatively prosperous and resourceful, and there was no loss of life from this famine. The land-tax of Madras, on the contrary, is heavy and is enhanced from time to time, and the people are poor and resourceless; when, therefore, a famine broke out there in 1877, five millions perished. A third famine in Northern India in 1878 cost the lives of 1,250,000 people; and during the famine of 1889 in Madras and Orissa the loss of life was very severe, but no official figures are available. In 1892, again, there was a famine in Madras, Bengal, Burma, and Rajputana, causing a heavy loss of life in Madras but none in Bengal. In 1897 famine swept over all Northern India, Bengal, Burma, Madras, and Bombay. The number of people on relief works alone rose to three millions in the worst months. Deaths were prevented in Bengal and elsewhere, but in the Central Provinces the death rate rose from an average of thirty-three per mille to sixty-nine per mille during the year. The famine of 1900 in the Punjab, Rajputana, the Central Provinces, and Bombay was the most widespread ever known in India. The number of persons relieved rose to six millions in the worst months. In Bombay, in the famine camps, so Sir A. P. Macdonnell, President of the Famine Commission, reported, the people "died like flies." "The results of the three famines within the last ten years (1891–1901), and of the increasing poverty of the people, are shown in the census taken in March, 1901. The population of India has remained stationary during the last ten years. There is a slight increase in Bengal, Madras, and Northern

India, while there is an actual decrease of some millions in Bombay, the Central Provinces, and the Native States affected by recent famines. In other words, the population of India to-day is less by some thirty millions than it would have been if the nominal increase of one per cent per annum had taken place during these ten years." *

Warren Hastings, who had succeeded Clive as Governor of Bengal, was made first Governor-General in 1772. Pitt's India Bill became a law in 1784. It removed the administration of the East India Company from the hands of directors and placed it under the control of the crown, thus compelling some reforms. Lord Cornwallis then became the successor of Warren Hastings. The policy of all of the governor-generals under the East India Company was to extend the British territory, to absorb the Native States by declaring war on the slightest pretence, to increase the revenue, and to drain the country of her resources. "The people of India have no votes, and are not even represented in the

* Indian Famines, by R. C. Dutt, p. 2.

Executive Councils of India. They have no voice in the matter of taxation or of expenditure. They have no share in the work of adjusting the finances of India. Taxation exceeds all reasonable limits in India, and the proceeds of the taxation are not all spent in India. A large sum, estimated between twenty and thirty millions in English money, is annually drained from India to this country (England). The disastrous results of this annual drain have been described by many English writers and administrators throughout the century which has just closed." * Sir Thomas Munro, for some time Governor of Madras, after forty years' experience in India, wrote in 1824: "They (natives of India) have no share in making laws for themselves; little in administering them, except in very subordinate offices; they can rise to no high station, civil or military; they are everywhere regarded as an inferior race, and more often as vassals or servants than as the ancient owners and masters of the country. . . . All the civil and military offices of any importance are now held by Euro-

* Indian Famines, by R. C. Dutt, p. 10.

peans, whose savings go to their own country." Mr. Frederick John Shore, of the Bengal Civil Service, wrote in 1837: "The halcyon days of India are over; she has been drained of a large proportion of the wealth she once possessed, and her energies have been cramped by a sordid system of misrule, to which the interests of millions have been sacrificed for the benefit of the few." Professor H. H. Wilson, the noted English historian, also says of the annual drain from India: "Its transfer to England is an abstraction of Indian capital for which no equivalent is given; it is an exhausting drain upon the country, the issue of which is paid by no reflux; it is an extraction of the life-blood from the veins of national industry, which no subsequent introduction of nourishment is furnished to restore." John Sullivan, at one time a Member of the Government of Madras and President of the Board of Revenue, writes thus in one of his reports: "As to the complaints which the people of India have to make of the present fiscal system, I do not conceive that it is the amount, altogether, that they have to complain of. I think that they have rather to complain of the application of that amount. Under their own dynasties, all the revenue that was collected in the country was spent in the country; but under our rule, a large proportion of the revenue is annually drained away, and without any return being made for it; this drain has been going on now for sixty or seventy years, and it is rather increasing than the reverse. . . . Our system acts very much like a sponge, drawing up all the good things from the banks of the Ganges, and squeezing them down on the banks of the Thames. . . . They (the people of India) have no voice whatever in imposing the taxes which they are called upon to pay, no voice in framing the laws which they are bound to obey, no real share in the administration of their own country; and they are denied those rights from the insolent and insulting pretext that they are wanting in mental and moral qualifications for the discharge of such duties." *

The British administrators, in the first part of the nineteenth century, did all they could to

* Report of the Select Committee, p. 402.

promote English industries at the sacrifice of Indian industries; for the policy of English administration in India is shaped, not by statesmen and philosophers, but by merchants, traders, and manufacturers, who are the voters of Great Britain. British manufactures were forced into India through the agency of the Company's Governor-General and commercial residents, while Indian manufactures were shut out from England by prohibitive tariffs, as the following table will show.

"Petitions were vainly presented to the House of Common against these unjust and enormous duties on the import of Indian manufactures into England. One petition against the duties on sugar and spirits was signed by some four hundred European and Indian merchants," * and it was rejected by the British Government in England. The policy of England was to make Great Britain independent of foreign countries for the raw material upon which her valuable manufactures depend, and to make India the producer of raw materials for English manufac-

* Economic History of India, p. 294.

TABLE OF TARIFFS.

	1812. Per Cent on Value.	1824. Per Cent on Value.	1832. Per Cent on Value.
Ornamental cane-work. . . .	71	50	30
Muslins.	27⅓	37½	10
Calicoes.	71⅔	67½	10
Other cotton manufactures.	27⅓	50	20
Goat's-wool shawls.	71	67½	30
Lacquered ware.	71	62½	30
Mats.	68⅓	50	20
Raw silk.	£2 13s 6d on value *plus* 4s per pound	4s per pound	1d per pound
Silk manufactures.	Prohibited	Prohibited	20 per cent on value
Taffetas or other plain or figured silks.	"	"	30 " " " "
Manufactures of silk.	"	"	20 " " " "
Sugar (cost price about £1 per cwt.).	£1 13s per cwt.	£3 3s per cwt.	£1 12s per cwt.
Spirits.	1s 8d per gallon *plus* 19s 1½d excise duty	2s 1d per gallon *plus* 17s 0½d excise duty	15s per gallon
Cotton wool.	16s 11d per 100 pounds	6 per cent	20 per cent

tories. The German economist, Frederick List, said: "Had they sanctioned free importation into England of Indian goods, the English manufactories would have come to a stand." * Thus, within fifty years, India was reduced from the state of a manufacturing to that of an agricultural country.

Cotton and silk fabrics, shawls and woolen fabrics, sugar, tobacco, rum, dyes, saltpetre, coffee, tea, steel, gold, iron, copper, coal, timber, opium, and salt,—all these, and grains of all kinds, India had traded with other nations, both Asiatic and European; but, under the pretence of free trade, England has now compelled the Hindus to receive the manufactured products of England free of duty, and has imposed prohibitive duties on Indian manufactures imported to England. No Indian industry of any kind has been encouraged by the British Government during the last one hundred and fifty years. And no less than two hundred and thirty-five articles were subjected to internal duties under the East India Company. Section 6 of the Cotton Duties Act of 1896 runs

* The National System of Political Economy, p. 42.

thus: "There shall be levied and collected at every mill in British India, upon all cotton goods produced in such mill, a duty at the rate of 3½ per centum on the value of such goods." And Mr. Dutt, in commenting upon this Act, says: "As an instance of fiscal injustice, the Indian Act of 1896 is unexampled in any civilized country in modern times. Most civilized governments protect their home industries by prohibitive duties on foreign goods. The most thorough of Free Trade Governments do not excise home manufactures when imposing a moderate customs duty on imported goods for the purposes of revenue. In India, where an infant industry required protection, even according to the maxims of John Stuart Mill, no protection has ever been given. Moderate customs, levied for the purposes of revenue only, were sacrificed in 1879 and 1882. Home-manufactured cotton goods, which were supposed to compete with imported goods, were excised in 1894. And home goods which did not compete with foreign goods were excised in 1896. Such is the manner in which the interests of an unrepresented nation are sacrificed." * This will give you a rough idea of how India has prospered in her economic condition during British rule.

A special law still exists under the English Government to provide laborers for the cultivation of tea in Assam. "A dark stain is cast on this industry by what is known as the 'slave-law' of India. Ignorant men and women, once induced to sign a contract, are forced to work in the gardens of Assam during the term indicated in the contract. They are arrested, punished, and restored to their masters if they attempt to run away; and they are tied to their work under penal laws such as govern no other form of labor in India. Hateful cases of fraud, coercion, and kidnapping, for securing these labourers, have been revealed in the criminal courts of Bengal, and occasional acts of outrage on the men and women thus recruited have stained the history of tea-gardens in Assam. Responsible and high administrators have desired a repeal of the penal laws, and have recommended that the tea-gardens should obtain workers from

* India in the Victorian Age, p. 543.

the teeming labor markets of India under the ordinary laws of demand and supply. But the influence of capitalists is strong; and no Indian Secretary of State or Indian Viceroy has yet ventured to repeal these penal laws, and to abolish the system of semi-slavery which still exists in India." *

Now let us see what is the present political condition of the Indian people: "The East India Company's trade was abolished in 1833, and the Company was abolished in 1858, but their policy remains. Their capital was paid off by loans, which were made into an Indian Debt, on which interest is paid from Indian taxes. The empire was transferred from the Company to the Crown, but the people of India paid the purchase-money." † In 1858 the public debt was seventy million pounds, which had been piled up by the East India Company during the one hundred years of their rule in India, while they were drawing tribute from India, financially an unjust tribute, exceeding 150 millions, not counting

---

* India in the Victorian Age, p. 352.

† Economic History of India, p. xii.

interest. Besides this, they had charged India with the cost of the wars in China, Afghanistan, and in other foreign countries. India, therefore, in reality owed nothing at the close of the Company's rule. Her Public Debt was a myth. On the contrary, there was a balance of over 100 millions in her favor out of the money that had been drawn from her. The administration of the Crown doubled this Public Debt in nineteen years, bringing it up to 139 million pounds in 1877, when the Queen became Empress of India. Over 40 millions sterling of this represented the cost of the Mutiny wars, which was thrown on the revenues of India. India was also made to pay a large contribution to the cost of the Abyssinian war of 1867. In 1900 the debt amounted to 224 millions sterling. The construction of railways by Guaranteed Companies or by the State, beyond the pressing needs of India and beyond her resources, was largely responsible for this increase. It was also largely due to the Afghan wars of 1878 and 1897.

India pays interest on this debt, which annually increases. Besides this, she pays for all the officers, civil and military, and a huge standing army, pensions of officers, and even the cost of the India Building in London, as well as the salary of every menial servant in that house. For 1901–2 the total expenditure charged against revenue was £71,394,282, out of which £17,368,-655 was spent in England as Home Charges, not including the pay of European officers in India, saved and remitted to England. These Charges were as follows:

1. Interest on Debt and Management of Debt	£3,052,410
2. Cost of Mail Service, Telegraph Lines, etc., charged to India	227,288
3. Railways, State, and Guaranteed (Interest and Annuities)	6,416,373
4. Public Works (Absentee Allowances, etc.)	51,214
5. Marine Charges (including H. M. Ships in Indian Seas)	173,502
6. Military Charges (including pensions)	2,945,614
7. Civil Charges (including Secretary of State's Establishment, Cooper's Hill College, Pensions, etc.)	2,435,370
8. Stores (including those for Defence Works)	2,057,934
Total	£17,368,655

The following, again, is a comparative table of salaries paid out:

	Natives.	Eurasians.	Europeans.	In Thousands of Rupees.		
				Total Salaries of Natives.	Total Salaries of Eurasians.	Total Salaries of Europeans.
Civil department.	55	10	1211	947	151	25,274
Military..........	1	1	854	12	11	13,268
Public works......	3	4	239	33	45	3,415
Incorporated local funds...........	1	..	9	10	...	113
	60	15	2313	1002	207	42,070

Besides these 105 officers drawing Rs., 10,000 a year or more are employed by the railway companies; they are all Europeans, and their salaries amount to 16 lacks and 28 thousand rupees (about $542,667). Among the officers, who are paid between Rs. 5000 and Rs. 10,000 a year, we find 421 natives in the civil department as against 1207 Europeans and 96 Eurasians. In the military department 25 natives are employed and 1699 Europeans and 22 Eurasians; while, in the Department of Public Works, there are 85 natives, as against 549 Europeans and 3 Eurasians.

Mr. Alfred Webb (late M.P.), who has studied the subject with care, says: "In charges for the

India Office (in London); for recruiting (in Great Britain, for soldiers to serve in India); for civil and military pensions (to men now living in England, who were formerly in the Indian service); for pay and allowances on furloughs (to men on visits to England); for private remittances and consignments (from India to England); for interest on Indian Debt (paid to parties in England); and for interest on railways and other works (paid to shareholders in England),—there is annually drawn from India, and spent in the United Kingdom, a sum calculated at from £25,000,000 to £30,000,000" (between $125,000,000 and $150,000,000).

It would have been bad enough if this drain had continued for a few years, or even for one year, but it began with the day when India came under England's power and has been kept up ever since. Of this Mr. Brooks Adams writes: "Very soon after Plassey (fought in 1757) the Bengal plunder began to arrive in London, and the effect seems to have been almost instantaneous.... Possibly since the world began, no investment has ever yielded the profit reaped from the Indian plunder." * The stream of wealth ruthlessly drawn from the conquered people of India, and poured from Indian treasuries into English banks, between Plassey and Waterloo (fifty-seven years), has been variously calculated at from £500,000,000 to £1,000,000,000. The "Westminster Gazette" of London, April 24, 1900, estimates the drain from India to England, during the closing twenty-five years of the nineteenth century, to have been £500,000,000 ($2,500,000,000). It would be impossible to believe these enormous figures if they were not taken from authentic records. Can we wonder that India to-day is so impoverished? Could any nation withstand so merciless and unceasing a drain upon its resources?

The popular belief is, that England has sunk her enormous capital in the development of India; but the truth is, that England has not spent a cent in governing India. (Compare this with the Colonial Governments.) The Indian Government means to-day the government of a bureaucracy, which includes the Viceroy

* Law of Civilization and Decay, pp. 259–264.

and the Members of the Executive Council, the Commander-in-Chief, the Military Member, the Home Member, the Public Works Member, the Finance Member, and the Legal Member. The people are not represented in this Council; their agriculture, their landed interests, their trades and industries, are not represented; there is not, and never has been, a single Indian member in the Council. The members are high English officials, who draw large salaries and get pensions for life after their service is over.

Then in each large Indian province there is a Legislative Council, and some of the members of these smaller councils are elected under the Act of 1892. The principal function of the Legislative Council is legislation. In theory it exercises control over finance, but in practice the budget is submitted to the autocracy merely for criticism; the representatives, however, can exercise no control over its being passed.

The Council consists of twenty-five members, four of whom are Indians, recommended by certain constituencies but appointed by the Viceroy. He has the power to appoint any one he pleases. He calls them elected, for the purpose of argument. The four Indians sit at one end of the table and the Englishmen at the other end. Beginning with the Indians, each one reads the speech he has prepared in order of seniority, each speech being prepared without knowledge of what the others will say, consequently without reference to what they have said. There is no real discussion. The Viceroy may turn its course as he pleases. The representatives cannot produce any impression on the Council, nor can they divide the Council or shape the decision in any way. It is indeed no representation of the natives in the proper sense of the term.

The Viceroy of India is under the orders of the Indian Secretary of State, who is a member of the English Cabinet. The Secretary of State lives in England, six thousand miles away from the governed people. He is assisted by a Council of ten retired Anglo-Indian officials, who seek the interest of their own nation. The whole system is, as Sir William Hunter calls it, an "oligarchy" which does not represent the people.

The government of India is as despotic as it is in Russia, because three hundred millions of people who are governed have neither voice nor vote in the government. The interest of the British nation is the first aim of the present system of government. People pay heavy taxes of all kinds, and that is all. The government sends out expeditions to Soudan, Egypt, China, Tibet, and other places outside of India, and then the poor people of India are forced to pay the enormous cost of these expeditions, amounting to millions of dollars.* The land-tax, income tax, and various kinds of taxes are higher than in any other civilized part of the world. "In India the State virtually interferes with the accumulation of wealth from the soil, intercepts the incomes and gains of the tillers, and generally adds to its land-revenue demand at each recurring settlement, leaving the cultivators permanently poor. In England, in

* *Vide* India in the Victorian Age, p. 604.

Germany, in the United States, in France, and other countries, the State widens the income of the people, extends their markets, opens out new sources of wealth, identifies itself with the nation, grows richer with the nation. In India the State has fostered no new industries and revived no old industries for the people; on the other hand, it intervenes at each recurring land settlement to take what it considers its share out of the produce of the soil." *

"But the land-tax levied by the British Government is not only excessive, but, what is worse, it is fluctuating and uncertain in many provinces. In England, the land-tax was between one shilling and four shillings in the pound, i.e., between 5 and 20 per cent. of the rental, during a hundred years before 1798, when it was made perpetual and redeemable by William Pitt. In Bengal the land-tax was fixed at over 90 per cent. of the rental, and in Northern India at over 80 per cent. of the rental, between 1793 and 1822." †

* Economic History of British India, p. xi.

† *Ibid.* p. ix.

To-day the masses of people in India live on from two to five cents a day and support their families with these earnings. Expecting to have their grievances removed by the government, they have been agitating for the last twenty years by calling annual public meetings and special public meetings, where the best classes of educated people have been represented. Although the Indian Government has spared no pains to stop all such agitations, still the people have been passing resolutions and sending them to the Viceroy and to the Secretary of State. Not one single word of encouragement has ever come from the despotic rulers, who are determined to follow the steps of the Russians in their methods of administration. Indeed, Sir Henry Cotton says: "Even the Russian Government, which we are accustomed to look upon as the ideal of autocracy, is not such a typical autocracy as the Government of India."

Ambitious, unsympathetic young civilians go out to India for a few years to exploit the country, satisfy their greed and self-interest, and return home to live like lords, drawing upon the taxes of the impoverished millions. I will give you an illustration of Lord Curzon's administration. Lord Curzon was the most unpopular Viceroy ever in India. His policy was one of interference and distrust. He is no believer in free institutions or in national aspirations. He took away the freedom of the press, which was steadily gaining in weight and importance, by passing the Official Secrets Act. The policy of his administration was to keep all civil as well as all military movements of the government secret. He sent the expedition to Tibet. He wasted the resources of the country on the vain show and pomposity of the Durbar while millions were dying of famine and plague. He condemned the patriotic and national spirit of the Indians, and lastly he carried out the Roman policy of divide and rule by partitioning the Province of Bengal, simply to cripple the unity of the educated natives, as also of seventy millions of inhabitants. All these and many acts he carried out with such despotism and high-handedness, against the unanimous opinion of seventy million people, that they were driven to boycott all English goods and manufactures. The fire of boycott has spread all over the country, like wildfire in a forest. The people have unanimously appealed to the Viceroy and to the Secretary of State again and again, but all the higher officials of India and England have turned deaf ears to them. It is to be hoped that this boycott will bring the English autocrats and despots to their senses.

The people of India are loyal and peace-loving, but they are discontented and impoverished after carrying for one hundred and fifty years the burden of an unsympathetic alien government. There would have been continuous rebellion and mutiny had they not so long depended upon passive resistance with the expectation that some day the famous proclamation of the late Queen Victoria would be carried into effect. On the morrow of the dark mutiny Queen Victoria proclaimed:

"We desire no extension of our present territorial possessions; and, while we will permit no aggression upon our dominions or our rights to be attempted with impunity, we shall sanction no encroachment on those of others. We shall respect the rights, dignity, and honor of Native Princes as our own; and we desire that they, as well as our own subjects, should enjoy that prosperity and social advancement which can only be secured by internal peace and good government.

"We hold ourselves bound to the Natives of our Indian territories by the same obligations of duty which bind us to all our subjects, and those obligations, by the blessing of Almighty God, we shall faithfully and conscientiously fulfil.

"Firmly relying ourselves on the truth of Christianity, and acknowledging with gratitude the solace of religion, we disclaim alike the right and the desire to impose our convictions on any of our subjects. We declare it to be our royal will and pleasure that none be anywise favored, none molested or disquieted, by reason of their religious faith and observances, but that all shall alike enjoy the equal and impartial protection of the law; and we do strictly charge and enjoin all those who may be in authority under us that they abstain from all interference with the religious belief and worship of any of our subjects, on pain of our highest displeasure.

"And it is our further will that, so far as may be, our subjects, of whatever race or creed, be freely and impartially admitted to offices in our service, the duties of which they may be qualified, by their education, ability, and integrity, duly to perform."

(Lord Curzon, however, openly declared that all Indians were disqualified by reason of their race.)

This proclamation was repeated by King Edward VII on the day of his coronation. But have the Anglo-Indian bureaucracy shown any desire to do the things which were promised by the late Empress and the present Emperor, King Edward? No.

People have now organized themselves, have sent delegates to England and America, and have awakened to the truth of what John Stuart Mill said: "The government of a people by itself has a meaning and a reality, but such a thing as government of one people by another does not and cannot exist. One people may keep another for its own use, a place to make money in, a human cattle farm for the profit of its own inhabitants."

The natives of India are now determined to stand on their own feet, but it is a hard problem for an enslaved nation to raise their heads while the dominant sword of a powerful alien government is held close to their necks. If the people of America wish to know what would have been the condition of the United States under British rule, let them look at the political and economic condition of the people of India to-day.

Well has it been said by Mr. Reddy, an English friend of India: "England, through her missionaries, offered the people of India thrones of gold in another world, but refused them a simple chair in this world." *

* India, Oct. 13, 1905.

V.

EDUCATION IN INDIA.

EDUCATION in India can be divided into four periods: The first, the pre-Buddhistic, or before the sixth century B.C.; the second, the Buddhistic period, from 500 B.C. to the tenth century A.D.; the third, the Mahometan; and the fourth, the period under British rule.

In order to get a correct idea of the education of a people, we must first be familiar with the civilization of that people, because the standard of education must go parallel with the culture and civilization of a nation. As we have already seen, the earliest civilization of the Hindus began in the Vedic period. History tells us that during that time the Indo-Aryans developed their voluminous scriptural works known as the Vedic literature, which consists of the Rig Veda, Yajur Veda, Sâma

Veda, and Atharva Veda, with their Brâhmanas, Âranyakas, and Upanishads. All these are in the Sanskrit language and are the most ancient Scriptures of the world. The Hindus of to-day consider these Vedas as revealed just as other nations believe in their Scriptures as revealed. Long before the art of writing was known these Vedas were studied, committed to memory, and taught from mouth to mouth. In those early days the study of these Sacred Scriptures formed the principal feature in the education of the boys and girls of the Brâhmins, Kshatriyas, and Vaishyas.

The life of a Hindu at that time was divided into four periods. The first was that of the student. The Aryan boys were initiated as students between the ages of eight and twelve. They then went to the teacher's house, remained there and studied the Vedas. As in this age the students of civilized countries live in the universities for several years, so in ancient times the Hindu boys used to leave their homes and stay with their teachers. Some lived with them for twelve years, some for twenty-four, others for thirty-six or forty-eight years, in accordance with their desire to master one, two, three, or four Vedas. When they had finished these years of study under various instructors and professors, the students returned to their homes, after making a handsome gift to their masters. According to Hindu custom, no teacher should ever sell his knowledge or receive any salary in return for his instruction, but the students were allowed to make presents to their masters at the close of their studies. Having returned home, they married and settled themselves as householders. Some, however, did not return, but devoted their whole life to the study of various Shâstras or sciences.

The main object of education at that time was the moral and spiritual culture of the soul, the attainment of God-consciousness and the knowledge of the various sacrifices that are described in the Vedas. Along with the Vedas the students had to learn the six *Vedângas* or limbs of the Vedas. These were regarded as the most important branches of Scriptural study. The first was *Shikshâ* or the science of phonetics, that is, the science which explains the correct pronunciation of the Sanskrit words and texts used in the Vedas. The second was *Chhanda*, or metre. The Vedic hymns have different metres, and one must be familiar with them in order to read or chant correctly. The scholars and professors of Sanskrit in Europe and America find great difficulty in pronouncing Sanskrit words and sentences because their tongues are not flexible enough to express the minute shades of difference that exist in the sounds of Sanskrit words. The Hindus, however, used to study metre, as also the science of pronunciation and grammar. At that time (even as early as 1400 B.C.) they had a scientific grammar. The Greek and Sanskrit languages have the best grammars, but the Sanskrit is the most perfect grammar that exists in the world. Then *Nirukta*, the fourth branch, was the science which describes the etymology, the meanings of different words, as well as the use of the same word in various senses. Also there was *Kalpa*, which includes *Shrauta-sutras*, or the laws about sacrifices, *Dharma-sutras*, or laws regarding the duties of a true citizen, *Grihya-sutras*, the rules of domestic life, and *Sulva-sutras*, the geometrical principles for constructing sacrificial altars. And the last branch was *Jyotisha*, or astronomy. In order to fix the time for Vedic sacrifices they had to study astronomy. Without knowing astronomy they could not understand the Vedas and could not perform any of the sacrifices. For this reason we find many astronomical references in the Vedas.

These were the main branches of study to which every Hindu belonging to the upper three classes—Brâhmins, Kshatriyas, and Vaishyas—was entitled. Besides this private education in the house of some teacher, who, as I have already said, took no salary, there were public places for instruction. The courts of the enlightened kings and Mahârâjahs were the principal seats of learning where education was bestowed free of charge; and there were also the *Parishads*, which corresponded to the universities of Europe. "At the period of transition from the Vedic to the Brahmanic stage of religious development about 1200 B.C. the courts of the kings were the centers of culture. . . . At a later period, 1000 B.C., there arose Brahmanic settlements, called *Parishads*, which we might call *collegiate* institutions of learning." * These public institutions were started and established by Brâhmin professors and scholars. The students in them used to stay with the teachers and do some work in their households in return for free board and tuition. Professor Max Müller, in his "History of Sanskrit Literature," says that a "*Parishad* used to consist of 21 Brâhmins well-versed in philosophy, theology, and law. Sometimes three or four learned Brâhmin scholars would form a small *Parishad* in a village." In the Upanishads we find mention of this kind of ancient Hindu university system. For instance, in the Brihadâranyaka Upanishad, VI, 2, we read that Svetaketu went to the *Parishads* of the Panchâlas for education.

In these colleges were taught the Vedas, philosophy, theology, and Hindu law, civil and criminal,—law of agriculture, of property, of usury, laws of inheritance and partition. These

* Education in India, W. I. Chamberlain, Ph.D., p. 20.

laws still govern Hindu society even under British rule. England has not succeeded in changing the Hindu laws and has not found any others more just or more perfect than those of the Hindus. This is not an exaggeration. Students of law, who have studied Roman and European law for years, cannot complete their course without studying Hindu law.

I have already shown in the first lecture that there were six schools of philosophy among the Hindus of the pre-Buddhistic period, that is, between 1400 and 600 B.C. These six schools of philosophy included logic, psychology, the science of numbers and the evolution theory of Kapila, the atomic theory of Kanâda, the science of thought, metaphysics, and the monistic science and philosophy of Vedanta. The students received instruction in these various branches in the Parishads or universities. Arithmetic, Algebra, Geometry, Trigonometry, Decimal notation, and Astronomy were also taught during the pre-Buddhistic period. You may be surprised to know that in those ancient times such sciences and philosophies were known to the

Hindus; but it is a matter of history that these various branches of science and philosophy owed their origin to the Vedic religion of India. Geometry was developed from the rules for the construction of Vedic altars as described in the Vedas. For instance, it is told there to describe a circle, make a triangle, or inscribe a triangle in a circle, and so on. When geometry fell into disuse in the Buddhistic period, after sacrifices were no longer made, algebra took its place. "The science of algebra indeed received a remarkable degree of development in India; the application of algebra to astronomical investigations and to geometrical demonstrations is a peculiar invention of the Hindus; and their manner of conducting it has received the admiration of modern European mathematicians." *

Besides these, the great epics of Râmâyana and Mahâbhârata, which contain the ancient national history of the Hindus as well as the essence of all Hindu sciences and philosophies, came into existence during the pre-Buddhistic

* Civilization in Ancient India, Vol. II, p. 246.

period. They were studied by all classes of people, both men and women. They were written especially for those classes who were not fitted for Vedic studies. The Vedas and the various sciences and philosophies existed among the Hindus long before the art of writing was known in the world. Can you believe that the hundreds of volumes which have been handed down to us were originally learned and taught from memory? They were transmitted from generation to generation by word of mouth. What a marvellous memory the people of that time had! The Mahâbhârata, for example, contains one hundred thousand verses in Sanskrit, and when I was in India I knew a Brâhmin lady who could recite every sentence from the beginning to the end; and there are many scholars who can recite a volume with its commentary without looking at the book. All sciences and philosophies were originally written in Sanskrit, but lately they have been translated into the various spoken dialects, of which there are at present about one hundred and fifty in India. Through these the masses obtain their moral and spiritual training. Public lectures and readings are given in almost every Hindu village for the education of the illiterate classes. Even to-day, in all Hindu communities, this old system of reading a Sanskrit verse and then explaining it in the vernacular language is very common. Those who cannot read or write receive moral and spiritual instruction through these *Kathakatâ*, or public readings.

There were also medical schools for the study of *Âyurveda*, or the medical science. The word "Âyus" means life, and "veda" means wisdom, knowledge, and hence science. Âyurveda, therefore, is the "science of life." It contains the Hindu *materia medica*, which is much older than the sixth century B.C. It was taught long before the time of Hippocrates, the "father of medicine," who lived about 400 B.C. Even in that early pre-Buddhistic age, Hindu medicine received scientific treatment, and there were separate schools and colleges for medical students. During the Buddhistic period, medical science made considerable progress, and exhaustive scientific works were written on medicine. Among these, the works by Charaka and Sushruta were the best. Their writings became so widely known that translations of them were already familiar to the Arabs in the eighth century A.D., at the time of Haroun-al-Raschid; and they still remain to-day the standard medical works among Hindu physicians. They contain exhaustive chapters on anatomy and physiology; on symptoms, diagnoses, and causes of various diseases, and on their proper treatment. Their words may be archaic, but they give a scientific treatment which was unknown in any other part of the world at that time.

Chemistry, in Sanskrit "Rasâyana," was also familiar to the Hindus from very early times. "Nor is this surprising, as the materials for preparing many chemical products have abounded in India. Rock-salt was found in Western India; borax was obtained from Tibet; saltpetre and sulphate of soda were easily made; alum was made in Cutch; and sal ammonia was familiar to the Hindus; with lime, charcoal, and sulphur they were acquainted from time immemorial. The alkalies and acids were early known to the

Hindus, and were borrowed from them by the Arabians. The medicinal use of metals was also largely known. We have notices of antimony and of arsenic, of medicines prepared with quicksilver, arsenic, and nine other metals. The Hindus were acquainted with the oxides of copper, iron, lead, tin, zinc, and lead; with the sulphurets of iron, copper, antimony, mercury, and arsenic; with the sulphates of copper, zinc, and iron; with the diacetate of copper and the carbonates of lead and iron." * Dr. Royle also says, in his essay on "Hindu Medicine": "Though the ancient Greeks and Romans used metallic substances as external applications, it is generally supposed that the Arabs were the first to prescribe them internally. . . . But in the works of Charaka and Sushruta, to which, as has been proved, the earliest of the Arabs had access, we find numerous metallic substances directed to be given internally." † History tells us that Alexander the Great kept Hindu physicians in his camp for the treatment of diseases which

* Civilization in Ancient India, Vol. II, p. 254.

† Royle, p. 45.

Greek physicians could not heal; and in the eighth century A.D. the Mahometan Badshaw, Haroun-al-Raschid, retained in his court two Hindu physicians. As early as 260 B.C. the Buddhist emperor Asoka also established many public hospitals, not only for men, women, and children, but also for animals.

Megasthenes, after his long residence at the court of Chandra Gupta in the fourth century B.C., testified that he found among the Hindus various kinds of schools suited to the different castes. There were Brâhmin schools, whose function was to train priests and teachers; warrior schools, where the pupils received military training; industrial schools for the merchant class; and schools for the lowest caste, where manual labor was taught.

During the Buddhistic age, and before the Mahometan invasion, Hindu culture in every branch of science and philosophy made tremendous progress. Ârya Bhatta, the noted Hindu astronomer, who lived about 476 A.D. and who is called the Newton of India, wrote many works on algebra and astronomy. It was he who first discovered the rotation of the earth on its own axis. As a Jewish writer says: "The theory that the earth is a sphere revolving on its own axis, which immortalized Copernicus, was previously known only to the Hindus, who were instructed in the truth of it by Âryabhatta in the first century before the common era." * He also discovered the true cause of solar and lunar eclipses, and it was he who, for the first time, grasped the idea of gravitation toward the center (called in Sanskrit *Mâdhyâkarshan*, that is, attraction towards the center), and correctly calculated the distance of the earth's circumference. His successor, Varâhamihira, another noted astronomer (500–587 A.D.), left valuable works, especially his "Brihat Sanhitâ," which covered almost every department of natural history and was encyclopedic in its nature. Brahma Gupta, who lived in 628 A.D., described in his astronomical system the true places of the planets, the calculation of lunar and solar eclipses, and wrote a treatise on spherics. There are

* Jewish Encyclopedia, Vol. XII, p. 689.

still some ruins of Hindu observatories in Benares and other cities.

In the sixth century A.D., this golden age of science and letters reached its climax in the reign of the great Hindu emperor, Vikramâditya, who was what Augustus was to the Romans, what Alfred was to the English, what Charlemagne was to the French, what Asoka was to the Buddhists, and what Haroun-al-Raschid was to the Mahometans. He was the great supporter of learning and education among the Hindus. To the learned, to the illiterate, to poets, to story-tellers, to dramatists and novelists, to astronomers, lexicographers, and historians, to the old and to the young, the name of Vikramâditya is as familiar in India as the name of any great patron of science, drama, poetry, and education of modern Europe. He had nine gems in his court, and the finest among them was Kalidâsa, the great Hindu dramatist. He was as great as Shakespere of England; indeed, he is called the Shakespere of India. His best-known drama, "Sakuntalâ," has been translated into more than one European language, and has been considered by such great scholars as Augustus William Von Schlegel, Alexander Von Humboldt, and Goethe as one of the dramatic masterpieces of the world. Goethe speaks thus of it:

"Wouldst thou the life's young blossoms and the fruits of its decline,
And all by which the soul is pleased, enraptured, feasted, fed,—
Wouldst thou the earth and heaven itself in one sweet name combine?
I name thee, O Sakuntalâ, and all at once is said."

You have heard something about "Sakuntalâ," "Vikramorvasi," and the other dramas and masterpieces which Kalidâsa left. His "Megha-duta," or the "Cloud Messenger," can stand side by side with the best poems of Shelley and Wordsworth, if not higher. One critic says: "Like Wordsworth, he looked upon Nature with the eye of a lover, and his knowledge of the physical laws is superior to that of any other Hindu poet." Kalidâsa's successors,—Bhâravi, Dandin, Bânabhatta, Subandhu, Bhartrihari, Bhavabhuti,—all these great Hindu poets and dramatists lived in the sixth century A.D. Their writings are still studied in all Sanskrit colleges, as they were twelve centuries ago.

The fables of Panchatantra and of Hitopadesha,* which gave foundation to Æsop's fables and to the fables of Pilpay, are also still studied in the primary schools of India. They came into existence in the sixth century after Christ, and have been translated into all the civilized languages of the world. Panchatantra "was translated into Persian in the reign of Nausharwan (531–572 A.D.). . . . The Persian ranslation was rendered into Arabic, and the Arabic translation was rendered into Greek by Symeon Seth about 1080. . . . A Spanish translation of the Arabic was published about 1251. The first German translations were published in the fifteenth century."† Besides these, the vast literature known as the "Purânas" is still studied by all classes of people, both men and women, as they were a thousand years ago.

From this you will get an idea of the civiliza-

* The fables of Hitopadesha have been translated by Sir Edwin Arnold under the name of "The Book of Good Counsels."

† Civilization in Ancient India, Vol. II, p. 297.

tion of the Hindus during the ancient pre-Buddhistic and mediæval ages, and you will be able to form some conception of what kind of education they received before the advent of the British in India. The Hindus, it must be remembered, have gone through a great many national disasters, calamities, and vicissitudes; and during the Mahometan occupation, which began in the eleventh century A.D. and continued for nearly six hundred years, they made very little progress in scientific education. They had to fight to protect themselves against the invaders, and turn their attention to their political condition; consequently they neglected the study of science. Furthermore, the Mahometan sword and fire destroyed the glorious monuments of Hindu culture and civilization. The Mahometan rulers never encouraged any kind of study outside of the reading of the Koran, for which classes were attached to the mosques. It is said that the Mogul Emperor Arangzeb, in the seventeenth century, established universities in all the principal cities and erected schools in the smaller towns, but it is now difficult to get any historical evidence to support this statement. A Mahometan believes that the essence of all literature and of all science is summed up in the Koran, so nothing outside of the Koran is to be studied. If all that is worth knowing is in the Koran, then there is no use of studying any other books. So they destroyed all the Scriptures, and all the works on science and philosophy, which they could get hold of. But the caste prejudice of the Hindus kept the Brâhmins from mixing with the Mahometans, and one of the most beneficial effects of the caste system was the preservation of the Sacred Books of the Hindus from the destructive hands of fanatical Mussulmans.

Mahometan elementary schools were started for the study of the Persian and Arabic languages. Many Hindu boys used to study these languages in Mahometan schools. They had no feeling of prejudice, so far as education was concerned. In the advanced Mahometan schools, there were complete courses in rhetoric, logic, law, ritual, and theology; all these and the Arabic language were taught to Mussulman students, but not to the Hindus. Euclid and Ptolemy's astronomy, and other branches of natural philosophy, were also taught in the high schools for Mahometans at the time when British rule began in India, about the middle of the eighteenth century.

The pioneers of Western education in India were the Christian missionaries. Some Danish missionaries arrived at Tranquebar, in Southern India, in 1706, and at once began to study the vernacular languages in order to teach the Bible. They founded some schools for that purpose, which were of minor importance. Their object was to convert the students to Christianity. In 1727 the first English mission established in India a society for promoting Christian knowledge, but it did not make much progress until the beginning of the nineteenth century, when the third missionary society of the English Baptists was established in Bengal. Their representatives were Carey and Marshman, who were men of ability and distinction. They studied the vernacular languages, and established schools for the teaching of the Bible.

The East India Company, however, hesitated to impart English education to the natives of India. When, in 1792, Wilberforce proposed to add two clauses to the Charter Act of the year for sending out schoolmasters to India, the directors of the Company strongly objected to the proposal. "On that occasion one of the Directors stated that we had just lost America from our folly in having allowed the establishment of schools and colleges, and that it would not do for us to repeat the same act of folly in regard to India; if the natives required anything in the way of education they must come to England for it." * This policy still exists at the bottom of the educational system established by the British Government in modern India. Although this policy, or rather fear, has apparently been modified, and schools, colleges, and universities have been founded, still the government of India does not feel safe in giving the natives substantial higher education of the same nature as can be obtained in England,

* J. C. Marshman's Evidence, Lords' Second Report, 1853.

Europe, or America. It was on account of this fear that the only educational institutions which were established up to 1792 were a Mahometan College at Calcutta, founded by Warren Hastings in 1781, and a Sanskrit College at Benares, founded by Lord Cornwallis in 1792. The main object of these institutions was to train law officers, both Mahometan and Hindu, to help the English judges in the judicial administration of the country. For twenty years longer the English Government was disinclined to spread English education in India.

In 1813 the British Parliament, for the first time, offered the sum of £10,000 from the revenue of India, to be appropriated for the education of the people of the three provinces of Bengal, Bombay, and Madras. Nothing, however, was done for ten years until 1823.* In the meantime the Hindus themselves, under the leadership of the great Hindu reformer, whose name is known all over the world, Râjah Râm Mohun Roy, became anxious to learn the English lan-

* *Vide* Sir Charles Trevelyan's Evidence, Lords' Second Report, 1853.

guage. He was the first Hindu who learned English thoroughly by his private exertions, for there was no school at that time; and he was the first native of India who went to England, where he died. His grave still exists in Bristol. At that time there was in Calcutta an illiterate English watchmaker, Mr. David Hare by name. He was a man of great energy and practical sense. Râjah Râm Mohun Roy consulted with him and planned to open an English seminary. The project started in 1815, and this energetic Mr. Hare had some circulars written out and distributed. He first succeeded in interesting some of the English officers and some representative Hindus, and in 1817 he established a school at Calcutta which is known to-day as the Hare School. It was the first respectable English seminary in Bengal, and was founded by the Hindus themselves before the British Government did anything for education in India.*

In 1820 the Government of India started an inquiry to find out the indigenous method of

* *Vide* Rev. Alexander Duff's Evidence, Lords' Second Report, 1853.

education among the Hindus in the Presidencies of Madras, Bombay, and Bengal; but for two years nothing was done. In 1822 Sir Thomas Munroe, the Governor of Madras, finding the decay of literature and arts and the deep ignorance of the masses, started an investigation, from which he discovered that the number of Hindu schools and colleges under the old Hindu system, in the Presidency of Madras alone, amounted to 12,498 among a population of something over twelve millions. In his report to the Court of Directors, which was made known in 1826, he says: "I am inclined to estimate the portion of the whole population who receive school education to be nearer one-third than one-fourth of the whole. The state of education exhibited, low as it is, compared with our own country, is higher than it was in most European countries at no very distant time." *

In 1823 Lord Elphinstone, Governor of Bombay, found that there was in the Bombay Presidency alone 1705 Hindu schools and colleges; and in 1835 Lord Bentinck discovered 3355

* Minute dated March 10, 1826.

Hindu schools among a population of seven millions in Bengal alone. This will prove how the Hindus have always cared for knowledge, culture, and education. In every village there was an elementary school where the village boys were taught reading, writing, arithmetic, and the elements of mensuration. These elementary schools were called *Pâthasâlâs*, or school-houses. Besides these, there were collegiate institutions like the *Parishads*, which I have already described, for higher education in grammar, mathematics, rhetoric, poetry, astronomy, and other branches of science and philosophy, as they were known to the Hindus at that time. The proportion of the latter to the former, that is, of collegiate schools to village schools, was one to three.

A Committee of Public Instruction was appointed by the East India Company's government in 1823, and the £10,000, which had been granted by Parliament ten years before, were expended in establishing an English school, under the name of Hindu College, in Calcutta, six Oriental colleges, and a number of elementary schools in Bengal and Rajputana. The Committee also gave its attention to the publication of Oriental books, and started a press in 1824.

Between 1823 and 1833 no special thing was done in the educational line other than to add classes in English in all the chief colleges. In 1835 Lord Bentinck, the Governor-General of India, enlarged the Committee of Public Instruction and appointed Macaulay as its president. Two distinguished Hindu gentlemen of the time, Sir Râjah Radha Kanta Deb Bahadur and Rossomoy Dutt of Calcutta, and Takawar Jung, the Mahometan Nawab of Bengal, were enrolled as members of the Committee. With Macaulay's support and assistance, Lord Bentinck passed the famous resolutions of March 7, 1835, by which the English language was established as the language of superior education in India. The resolutions were these:

(1) That the chief aim of the educational policy of the Government should be to promote a knowledge of European literature and science.

(2) That henceforth no more stipends should be conferred, but that all existing stipends

should be continued as long as the natives continue to avail themselves of them.

(3) That the printing of Oriental books should at once cease, and that the funds thus set free should be employed in promoting European studies through the medium of the English language.

In Madras, about this time, a Hindu named Pachiapa left a large donation for religious uses, and out of this sum, which amounted to nearly £80,000, a central educational institution, which is now known as Pachiapa's College, was established by the Hindus in 1839. It still continues to be the most flourishing college for the study of English in Madras, and it was the first college established there. In 1830 Alexander Duff arrived in Calcutta as the missionary of the General Assembly of the Scotch Kirk, and established a school which was at first a great success; but his aim was to convert the natives to Christianity, and when some of the students were persuaded to accept Christianity, the whole Hindu community protested against the object and plan of the missionary schools and would not allow their children to enter them as students. During his stay, Alexander Duff succeeded in converting only forty young Hindus who were studying in his school, and the conversion of these created a great sensation in the city of Calcutta. About that time the Hindus began to study Thomas Paine's "Age of Reason." The book spread like wildfire among native students and scholars, and Dr. Duff, finding that it was a great obstacle in the path of converting the Hindus, bought all the copies that were in the market, piled them in the street and made a bonfire out of them; but the Hindus reprinted the book and distributed it among themselves.

Being thus aroused, the native Hindus of Calcutta were determined to start schools and colleges for the education of their boys in English. Foremost among them was Pundit Iswara Chunder Vidyasâgar, the most distinguished educationalist and the greatest Hindu scholar of his time. He established by his own individual efforts, unaided by the Government, the Metropolitan School in Calcutta, and to-day it is one of the most powerful and best conducted colleges in India. It has always been entirely under Hindu management, and all its teachers and professors are Hindus. Hundreds and thousands of students study English and graduate every year under native professors.

Lord Hardinge established one hundred schools in the different districts of Bengal for the purpose of imparting education in the vernacular as a preliminary step to higher education in English. He also passed the famous resolution of 1844 for the selection of candidates for public employment from those who had been educated in the institutions established. This gave a tremendous impetus to native efforts to start schools, colleges, and seminaries in Calcutta and other places. Intense desire to learn and teach English was expressed by all classes of people and no caste distinction was observed. Students from all castes and all classes wanted to study and to teach English, and schools sprang up on all sides for imparting English education.

In 1836 Hoogly College was opened, and in three days twelve hundred names were enrolled and an auxiliary school was immediately filled.

In 1843 there were fifty-one schools and colleges, containing 8,200 students, of whom 5,132 were studying English, 426 Sanskrit, 572 Arabic, and 706 the Persian language. In 1839 Lord Auckland offered a grant from the Government treasury of 25,000 rupees (about $8000) to promote Oriental education; and in 1845 Mr. Thomason, the Governor of the Northwestern Provinces, started a plan to encourage the native village schools of the Hindus, which have existed in India for ages. This plan involved the establishment of: (1) An elementary school for circles of villages, each school to be situated in a central village and no village to be more than one mile from the central school; (2) A middle school at the headquarters of each subdivision; (3) A high school in each Zillah or district. This plan was sanctioned by the Directors, who made an allowance of 500,000 rupees. Operations began in 1850, and after four years there were eight District High Schools in the whole Northwestern Province. For the support of these state schools (which were not free) monthly fees, which varied from one to twelve rupees, were exacted of all students. In the state schools the fees were higher than in the private schools.

The missionary schools were mostly elementary or primary. Only three or four of them imparted secondary education, and some of them were free of charge to help the poorer classes. Up to this time the Government had not taken any step to educate the girls. Female education received no support from the Government; while the missionaries were trying their best to educate native girls in the tenets of Christianity, denouncing the religion of their forefathers and condemning everything of Hindu origin or which had to do with Hindu society and religion, in the same manner as they did in the schools for boys. This is one of the greatest drawbacks in the missionary methods of education. They condemn everything that is outside of their religion, their standards and their ideals. They are too narrow to see good in any but their own creed and dogmas. They do not consider the Hindu religion as a religion or the Hindu Saviours as Saviours; but they think that the Hindus are all going to eternal perdition and so they are very anxious to save their heathen souls! An American missionary, in referring to the schools for non-Christians in India, writes: "These are especially established with a view to reaching and affecting the non-Christian community. . . . They represent the leaven of Christianity in India. They furnish excellent opportunity to present Christ and his Gospel of salvation to a large host of young people under very favorable circumstances. . . . And I fearlessly maintain that more conversions take place and more accessions are made through these schools than through any other agency." This will give you an idea of the fanaticism and bigotry of these apostles of Christianity, who pretend to impart free education to the boys and girls of poor, illiterate parents. The poor Hindu boys and girls come to study and learn something, but instead of receiving the blessing of true education, their minds are filled with superstitious and unscientific doctrines and dogmas, and they are forced to leave the community of their parents and relatives and become converts to Christianity. These missionaries do not think for a moment why the Hindus should give up their own prophets and Saviours and worship the prophets of the Semitic race, especially of the Jews. Why should the Hindus abandon their ancient traditions and the religion of their Aryan forefathers? Why should they forsake the Aryan prophets and accept the Jewish prophets instead? Those who never had any higher philosophy, higher religion, or a spiritual leader like Christ, may accept with delight the banner of Christ, but not the Hindus, who have many Saviours,—Krishna, Râma, Buddha, Chaitanya, Râmakrishna,—each of whom, according to the Hindus, was as great as the Saviour of Nazareth. The Christian missionaries, before preaching Christ among the Hindus, should first convert the Jews.

The East India Company's charter was renewed in 1853, and a Lords' Committee was appointed to make necessary additions or modifications in the policy of the government of India. Among other things, the Committee discussed the subject of education of the people of India. After collecting evidence from all sides, the Committee issued a Despatch in 1854, constituting the great Charter of Indian education; and on this Despatch the whole system of education in India of to-day is based. It approved of the higher education and the establishment of universities in Calcutta, Bombay, and Madras, the chief towns of the three Presidencies under British rule. The Despatch of 1854 extended the field of education and prescribed these objects: "First, the constitution of a separate department of the administration of education. Second, the institution of the universities at the Presidency towns. Third, the establishment of institutions for training teachers for all classes of schools. Fourth, the maintenance of the existing Government colleges and high schools, and the increase of their number when necessary. Fifth, the establishment of new middle schools. Sixth, increased attention to vernacular schools, indigenous or other, for elementary education. And seventh, the introduction of a system of grants-in-aid."

"Aid is to be given (so far as available funds may render it possible) to all schools imparting a good secular education, provided they are under adequate local management and subject to Government inspection, and provided that fees, however small, are charged in them." In the assignment of these grants, however, there were no less than five systems in operation. They were as follows:

(1) The *Salary Grant System*, in use in Madras only, was applied to secondary education. Under this system the Government contributed a fixed proportion of the teacher's salary in accordance with his qualifications.

(2) The *Results Grant System* was in Madras applied to primary education only, and in Bombay to secondary education. To obtain this grant it was necessary to pass Government examinations.

(3) The combined *Salary-Results System*.

(4) The *Fixed Period System* was in operation in the greater part of Northern and Central India. Under this an average grant was paid for periods of three or five years.

(5) The *Captitative System* was applied to a few girls' schools in Bengal.

The seven articles of the Despatch of 1854

helped in a systematic manner the promotion of education in India. The English language became the medium in the higher branches and the vernacular in the lower. The system of grants-in-aid was based upon the principle of absolute neutrality. Aid was given from 1854 to all schools imparting a good secular education. Three universities were established in 1857 by Lord Canning after the model of the London University. Thus the inspiring influence of Western education reached a larger circle of the population. Two more universities have been added since,—one in the Punjab in 1882 and the other in Allahabad in 1887; so there are altogether five universities in India,—one in Calcutta, one in Bombay, one in Madras, one in the Punjab and the other in Allahabad. These universities consist of a chancellor, the governor of the Presidency *ex officio*, a vice-chancellor, and not less than thirty fellows, who constitute a Senate. The Senate controls the management of the funds of the universities, and frames rules and regulations, which are subject to Government approval and under which examinations are held periodically in the various branches of art and science by examiners chosen from among themselves or nominated from outside. The Senate is divided into four faculties,—Arts, Law, Medicine, and Engineering. The executive government of the university is in the hands of a syndicate, which consists of the vice-chancellor and eight of the Fellows. This syndicate selects examiners, regulates examinations, recommends for degrees, honors, and rewards, and carries on the business of the university. Boards of studies in the various departments are also appointed from among the Fellows by the syndicate. The Fellows do not correspond to the Fellows of this country, nor of Europe, nor even of England. The office of Fellow is an honorary office, usually conferred on some representative man or upon those who have been active in the cause of education. They may be natives or Europeans. The Indian universities are without a staff of teachers. They simply hold examinations and grant degrees, but they have no courses of lectures. In India we do not have anything like the universities of this country and nothing like Cambridge and Oxford. I will give you an idea of the examinations that are held under the universities:

The subjects of examinations are: (1) English; (2) A classical (Oriental or European) or vernacular language; (3) Physics and Chemistry; (4) History; (5) Geography; (6) Arithmetic, Algebra, Geometry. This is the examination for entrance into college. Under each university there are many schools and colleges started and managed by the natives. Then after two years' study in a college the student prepares for the First Examination in Arts. The subjects are: (1) English; (2) A classical language (Oriental or European) or a vernacular; (3) Logic; (4) Mathematics; (5) History and Geography; and (6) Physical Science. Two years later comes the B.A. Examination. This has two branches—the Language Division and the Science Division. The subjects in the Language Division are: (1) English; (2) A classical or vernacular language; (3) Mathematics; (4) and (5) any two of the following: Moral Philosophy, History, and Advanced Mathematics. The Science Division consists of (1) English; (2) Mathematics; (3) Chemistry; (4) Physical Geography; (5) either Physics, Physiology, or Geology.

For the degree of Masters of Arts there is an honor examination in Language, Mental and Moral Philosophy, Natural Science, or History and Mathematics. Then there are Law examinations, Medical examinations, and Civil Engineering examinations with degrees.

This system has been in existence for the last forty-eight years. The total number of students in schools and colleges all over British India is 4,405,042. To-day, excluding cities, three villages out of four are without schools, and seven children out of eight are growing up in ignorance and darkness. According to the census of 1901 there are 147,086 educational institutions of all kinds in British India. Of these 104,743 are public institutions (that is, institutions open to all classes but not free), which are divided as follows: 44 Professional Colleges, 141 Art Colleges, 5461 Secondary Schools, 98,133 Primary Schools, 170 Training

Schools, and 494 Special Schools. In addition to these there are 42,343 private institutions, of which 4306 are advanced, 26,668 elementary, 11,016 teaching the Koran only, and 263 not conforming to departmental standards. "During the past three years the sum of 4,000,000 rupees has been contributed by the (native) public in the United Provinces towards education. Nearly half of this sum was given in the year 1905. The numbers attending public institutions of all kinds have increased, while those attending private institutions have declined. The past year witnessed the erection of several schools and boarding-houses, the institution of schemes for the development of Sanskrit, Arabic, the enlargement of the Medical School at Agra, the development of mechanical training and electrical work at Rurki and the starting of an institution for mechanical and manual training at Lucknow." *

The Government does not give free education in India and although the Hindus pay all kinds of taxes—40 per cent more than the tax-

* The Indian Nation, Jan. 22, 1906.

payer of Great Britain and Ireland—and support the most expensive system of administration, still they do not receive from the Government free education. The Government now spends annually nearly 27 million pounds sterling for military expenses and about £750,000 for the education of the natives. The Rev. J. T. Sunderland, after long residence in India, says: "Much credit has been given to the Indian Government for education. It has done some good work in this direction, for which let it have full praise. But how little has it done compared with the need, or compared with what the people want, or compared with its ability, if it would only use its resources primarily for India's good! Why has so little of the people's money been spent for education? In the schools of India, of all kinds, high and low, there are some 4,418,000 scholars (if we include the native states). But what is this number in a population nearly as large as that of all Europe? How much does the Indian Government spend annually for education? The munificent sum of one penny and a fifth per head of the population! Think of it! Is it any wonder that, after a century and a half of British dominance, the number of persons in India who can read and write is only about eleven in a hundred among males, and one in two hundred among females? With their native industries so badly broken down, the Indian people have special need for industrial, technical, and practical education. But their rulers are giving them almost nothing of this kind. Britain's neglect of education is a dark stain upon her treatment of India." *

The Government has no school or college for female education. The first girls' school was established in Calcutta by Mr. Drinkwater Bethune (a legal member of the Governor-General's Council), who gave £10,000 from his own pocket. This school is the most successful institution for girls in India, and teaches up to the highest grades of university examinations. The Indian universities bestow degrees on women, and lady graduates take their degrees in Calcutta, Madras, and Bombay. There are

* Paper on "The Causes of Famines in India," before the Canadian Institute, p. 22.

many girls' schools which have been started by the Hindus. In private primary schools, little boys and girls are taught together. The total number of girls who receive education is about half a million; but the majority of Hindu girls receive their education at home. The illiterate women in India are given moral and spiritual instruction, as well as instruction in religious truths and moral duties, and in their national traditions and literature, to a much larger extent than in Europe.

About 85 per cent of the population of India to-day depends upon agriculture. Yet the Government had no agricultural institution in the country until recently, when it started one agricultural college in Poona, near Bombay.

Education in India is very expensive, considering that the average annual income per head is £2, out of which from 14 to 15 per cent goes towards paying taxes. Furthermore, the educated Hindus, who have spent a considerable part of this income in receiving university degrees, have no prospect of obtaining higher positions in Government offices. All the higher positions are occupied by English officials, who draw large salaries, while native graduates are allowed to remain as clerks on a salary of from three to ten dollars per month. Until recently, these Hindu graduates had the one chance of entering Government offices through competitive examinations. But Lord Curzon closed that door by passing the University Bill, which brings the universities and schools under rigid official control. Now none but those who are appointed by the Government can hold any Government position. The Official Secrets Bill passed by Lord Curzon has also gagged the Indian press. There are a number of daily and weekly papers published in English by the Hindus. But they cannot agitate the political and economic policy of the Government. Thus people are kept in absolute darkness. Notwithstanding his despotic rule, however, Lord Curzon did on· good act in allowing a permanent grant of £220,000 from the surplus revenue for primary education.

India needs to-day free education, and free industrial and technical schools and colleges for the masses. India needs schools and colleges for the education of girls, not under the management of Christian missionaries, but under the management of the Hindus. India needs a national university where boys and girls will receive secular education free of charge, and where all technical and manual training can be obtained freely.

To-day the Hindus have shown to the world that intellectually they are equal to the most intellectual people of Europe and America, but they are downtrodden and poor. The whole weight of the British Government is grinding the nation and crushing the spirit of progress. Furthermore, India is impoverished under British rule; yet the Hindus are raising private funds and sending their students to America and Japan to receive better and more substantial education than what they receive under the British Government. The Hindus are eager to learn, and they are indebted to England for introducing Western education in India. If England has done any good to India, it is by the introduction of English education. This is the greatest blessing that India has received under British rule.

The seed of Western education is sown in the soil of India; future generations will reap the fruit.

Herbert Spencer says "education is training for completeness of life." The Hindus now see the defects of the present system of education in India, and are endeavoring to reform it and to make it as perfect as it is in this land of free education and political independence. May their noble efforts be crowned with glorious success!

VI.

THE INFLUENCE OF INDIA ON WESTERN CIVILIZATION, AND THE INFLUENCE OF WESTERN CIVILIZATION ON INDIA.

THE dawn of Aryan civilization broke for the first time on the horizon, not of Greece or Rome, not of Arabia or Persia, but of India, which may be called the motherland of metaphysics, philosophy, logic, astronomy, science, art, music, and medicine, as well as of truly ethical religion. Although students in the schools and colleges of modern Europe and America are generally taught that the Greeks and Romans were the fathers of European civilization and that philosophy and science first arose in ancient Greece, still it has been proved by the Oriental scholars of Europe and by all impartial students of history that ancient Greece was greatly indebted to India for many of her best ideas in philosophy, science and intellectual culture, as also for many of her ethical and spiritual ideals.

If we read the writings and historical accounts left by Pliny, Strabo, Megasthenes, Herodotus, Porphyry and a host of other ancient authors of different countries, we shall see how highly the civilization of India was regarded by them. In fact, between the years 1500 and 500 B.C., the Hindus were so far advanced in religion, metaphysics, philosophy, science, art, music, and medicine that no other nation could stand as their rival, or compete with them in any of these branches of knowledge. On the contrary, many of the nations which came in contact with the Hindus through trade or otherwise, accepted the Hindu ideas and moulded their own after the Hindu pattern. For instance, the science of geometry, as I have already said, was first invented in India by the Hindus from the Vedic rules for the construction of sacrificial altars; from these rules they gradually developed geometry, and it has been admitted by the great scholars that the world owes its first lesson in this science, not to Greece, but to India. The geometrical theorem that the square of the hypotenuse of a rectangular triangle is equal to the squares of its sides was ascribed by the Greeks to Pythagoras, but it was known in India at least two centuries before Pythagoras was born. It was contained in the two rules: "(1) The square of the diagonal of a square is twice as large as that square; and (2) The square of the diagonal of an oblong is equal to the square of both its sides." These rules formed a part of the Sulva Sutras, which date from the eighth century before Christ. There is a Greek tradition that Pythagoras visited India, and most probably he did, because in his writings we find such ideas as were very common among the Hindus, but which were unknown to other nations. Probably he learned from the Hindus his first lessons in geometry, mathematics, the doctrine of pre-existence and transmigration of souls, and of final beatitude, ascetic observances, prohibition of eating flesh, vegetarianism, the conception of the virtue of numbers, and lastly, the idea of a fifth element, which was unknown in Greece and Egypt at that ancient time. The Egyptians and

Greeks admitted four elements, but ether as an element was known only among the Hindus of those days. All these things were taught by the Hindus centuries before the time of Pythagoras. Prof. E. W. Hopkins admits this in his "Religions of India," as you will recall from the first lecture, when he says: "Before the 6th century B.C. all the religious-philosophical ideas of Pythagoras are current in India."

Geometry gradually fell out of use among the Hindus, and geometrical truths were represented by algebra and arithmetic. The Greeks could not rival the Hindus in the science of numbers. The world indeed owes decimal notation to India. The Arabs first learned it from the Hindus and then introduced it into Europe. It was unknown to the Greeks and Romans, and arithmetic as a practical science would have been impossible without decimal notation. The Hindus have also given algebra (Vijaganita) to the Western world through the Arabs, who translated it in the eighth century A.D.; and Leonardo da Pisa first introduced it into Europe in the thirteenth century. So the world received its first lesson in algebra from India. The Hindus were also the first teachers of plane and spherical trigonometry. The great Indian mathematician, Bhâskarâ-chârya, who lived from 1114–1150 A.D., wrote exhaustive treatises * on all these subjects, and his works contain solutions of remarkable problems which were not achieved in Europe until the seventeenth and eighteenth centuries.† In astronomical observations, the Hindus were the first to fix the lunar mansions, lunar *Zodiac*, and the divisions of the constellations. The Chinese

* Those treating of algebra and arithmetic have been translated by Colebrooke, and the portion on spherical trigonometry has been translated by Wilkinson.

† "A striking history has been told of the problem to find x so that ax^2+b shall be a square number. Fremat made some progress towards solving this ancient problem, and sent it as a defiance to the English algebraists in the seventeenth century. Euler finally solved it, and arrived exactly at the point attained by Bhâskara in 1150. A particular solution of another problem given by Bhâskara is exactly the same as was discovered in Europe by Lord Brounker in 1657; and the general solution of the same problem given by Brahmagupta, in the seventh century A.D., was unsuccessfully attempted by Euler, and was only accomplished by De la Grange in 1767 A.D. The favorite process of the Hindus known as the *Kuttaka* was not known in Europe till published by Bachet de Mezeriac in 1624 A.D."—Civilization in Ancient India, Vol. II, p. 246.

and Arabs borrowed these from India. The Hindus first developed the science of music from the chanting of the Vedic hymns. The Sâma Veda was especially meant for music. And the scale with seven notes and three octaves was known in India centuries before the Greeks had it. Probably the Greeks learned it from the Hindus. It will be interesting to you to know that Wagner was indebted to the Hindu science of music, especially for his principal idea of the "leading motive"; and this is perhaps the reason why it is so difficult for many Western people to understand Wagner's music. He became familiar with Eastern music through Latin translations, and his conversation on this subject with Schopenhauer is probably already familiar to you.

The Western world, again, owes its first lesson in medicine to India. In the preceding lecture I gave proofs that Alexander not only had in his camp Hindu physicians, but that he preferred them to Greek physicians. Megasthenes, Nearchus, and Arrian spoke highly of the wonderful healing powers of the Hindu physicians.

In 1837 Dr. Royle, of King's College, London, wrote his celebrated essay on "Hindu Medicine," in which he showed that Hippocrates, the father of medicine, who lived in Greece in the fourth century B.C., borrowed his *Materia Medica* from India. Dr. Royle says, "We owe our first system of medicine to the Hindus."

Herodotus, who lived in the fifth century B.C., states that the Hindus were the greatest nation of that age. He also writes that the Hindus had trade with Egypt, while from other sources we gather that they had trade with Babylon and Syria. From another authentic source we learn that there was a Hindu philosopher who visited Socrates at Athens, a fact which Prof. Max Müller confirms in his book on "Psychological Religion." This Hindu philosopher, we are told, had a conversation with the great Greek philosopher. He asked in what the philosophy of Socrates consisted, and Socrates replied that his philosophy consisted in inquiries about the life of man, upon which the Hindu philosopher smiled and answered: "How can you know things human without first knowing things divine?"

And that is an answer which could not have been given by any other than a Hindu, because the Hindus ascribed all true knowledge to Divine origin, and did not care much for the knowledge of anything human before knowing God.

Ralph Waldo Emerson says: "Plato was a synthesis of Europe and Asia, and a decidedly Oriental element pervades his philosophy, giving it a sunrise color." In fact, in teaching asceticism, Plato was more of a Hindu than a Greek, because, of all nations, the Greeks were least ascetic. My friend, Professor Edward Howard Griggs, in his lecture on the "Philosophy of Plato" before the Vedanta Society of New York, also admitted this in saying: "Plato's belief in the conquest of the senses, as the only means of attaining true knowledge, was preëminently Oriental and non-Greek." Moreover, if we study Plato carefully, comparing his ideas with those of the Upanishads and other Vedic writings, we find that his well-known figure of the man chained in the cave is merely an allegorical presentation of the Vedanta doctrine of Mâyâ, that the phenomenal world is like a dream;

while his other figure of the chariot was a favorite theme of the Vedic writers who lived centuries before Plato. In the Katha Upanishad, for instance, we read: "This body may be compared to a chariot, intellect to the charioteer, mind to the reins, the five senses to the horses, whose path is the object of senses." Sir William Jones, the first eminent Sanskrit scholar among the English, confirming this fact, writes that "it is impossible to read the Vedanta, or the many fine compositions in illustration of it, without believing that Pythagoras and Plato derived their sublime theories from the same fountain with the Indian sages." *

Professor Max Müller and other Oriental scholars maintain, as you know, that the logic of Aristotle was perhaps a Greek presentation of the Hindu logic. You will also remember that Professor Hopkins writes, in his "Religions of India," that Thales and Parmenides were both anticipated by the sages of India, while the Eleatic School appears merely a reflection of the Upanishads. He even suggests that the doc-

* Works (Calcutta Ed.), pp. 20, 125, 127.

trines propounded by Anaximander and Heraclitus might not have been known first in Greece. We should, indeed, bear in mind that after the invasion of India by Alexander the Great the connection between India and Greece became closer than ever before, and many Hindu philosophers lived at Athens and in other parts of Greece. They were known as Gymnosophists, or Hindu philosophers from India. At that time Alexandria became the center of trade and commerce between India and Greece, and there was great opportunity for interchange of ideas between the Hindus and Western nations. Porphyry speaks of the wise men from India in high terms of praise for their wisdom, morality, and knowledge of the mysteries of the universe. In regard to Neo-Platonism, Professor Garbe has said that Plotinus was in perfect agreement with the Hindu philosophers, and that his disciple Porphyry knew of the Yoga doctrine of union with the Deity. It was unknown to any of the Western nations, like the Hebrews, Parsees, or Egyptians. Through Plato and his followers, the Neo-Platonists, Stoics, and Philo of Alexandria were also influenced by the Hindu Philosophy. The idea of the *Logos* which formed the corner-stone of the philosophy of Plato, of the Neo-Platonists, of Philo, and later of the Fourth Gospel, first arose in India. In the Vedas we find reference to it; and it has moulded Hindu thought, as well as the religious ideals of other nations.

Christianity as a religion owes a great deal to India. This may startle some of our friends, but from the historical standpoint it is true. If we read the religious history of the East, we find many evidences which are undeniable. For instance, Asoka, who lived in 260 B.C., had his edicts inscribed on pillars of stone during his lifetime, and in one of those edicts we read that he sent Buddhist missionaries to different parts of the world, from Siberia to Ceylon, from China to Egypt, and that, for two centuries before the advent of Jesus, the Buddhist missionaries preached the sublime ethics of Buddha in Syria, Palestine and Alexandria. The same ethical ideas were afterwards repeated and emphasized by Christ. The Christian historian Mahaffi, speaking about those Buddhist missionaries, declared it to be a fact that they were the forerunners of Christ. These preachers influenced the Jewish sect known as the Essenes; and the Roman historian Pliny, who lived between 23 and 79 A.D., described the mode of living of the Essenes,—that they lived like hermits, without having any possessions or any sex relation, being celibates and associates of palm-trees. It can be shown that they belonged to the sect founded by the Buddhist monks from India, who lived in Syria, Palestine, and Egypt. Philosophers like Schelling and Schopenhauer, and Christian thinkers like Dean Mansel and D. Millman, admit that the sect of the Essenes arose through the influence of the Buddhist missionaries who came from India. Moreover, it is a well-known fact that John the Baptist was an Essene. Ernest Renan, speaking of John the Baptist, says: "He led there a life like that of a Yogi of India, clothed with skins or cloth of camel's hair, having for food only locusts and wild honey. . . . We might imagine ourselves transported to the banks of the Ganges, if special features had not revealed in this recluse the last descendant of the grand prophets of Israel." * Again he says: "The teachers of the young were also at times a species of anchorites, resembling to some extent the *Gurus* (spiritual preceptors) of Brâhminism. In fact, might there not in this be a remote influence of the *Mounis* (sages) of India? Perhaps some of those wandering Buddhist monks who overran the world, as the first Franciscans did in later times, preaching by their actions and converting people who knew not their language, might have turned their steps towards Judea, as they certainly did towards Syria and Babylon. . . . Babylon had become for some time a true focus of Buddhism. Boudasp (Bodhisattva) was reputed a wise Chaldean, and the founder of Sabeism. Sabeism was, as its etymology indicates, *baptism*." † And he continues: "We may believe, at all events, that many of the external practices of John, of the Essenes, and of the Jewish spiritual teachers of this time, were derived from influences then but recently received from the far East. The fundamental practice which gave to

* Life of Jesus, p. 126. † *Ibid.*, p. 127.

the sect of John its character, and which has given him his name, has always had its center in lower Chaldea, and constitutes a religion which is practised there to this day. This practice was baptism or total immersion. Ablutions were already familiar to the Jews, as they were to all the religions of the East. The Essenes had given them a peculiar extension." *

Thus we see that baptism by water was introduced among the Essenes by the Buddhist missionaries, having originated in India. Baptism afterwards became the principal ceremony at the time of the initiation of the disciple in the religion of John. The life of Jesus the Christ as described in the Synoptic Gospels,—the immaculate conception of a virgin mother, the miraculous birth, the story of the slaughter of infants by Herod, and the chief events of his life, all these seem like repetitions of what happened in the lives of Krishna (1400 B.C.) and of Buddha (547 B.C.). In fact, the idea of the incarnation of God is purely a Hindu idea. It was not known among the Jews. The Jews never accepted

* Renan, Life of Jesus, p. 128.

Christ as the incarnation of Divinity, but from the Vedic period the Hindus accepted many Avatâras or Incarnations of the Lord in a human form, and this is at the foundation of the religion of the Hindus. Many of the famous parables of Jesus the Christ existed among the Hindus and Buddhists of the pre-Christian era. In the Gospel of Buddha, for instance, we find the parables of the prodigal son and of the marriage feast, which were taught by Buddha to his disciples about five centuries B.C., and they resemble in every way the similar parables of Jesus the Christ. The Roman Catholics have taken a great many of their ideas—their form of worship, the monastic life, the nunnery and the idea of purgatory—from the Buddhists of India. In the religious history of the world, Buddha was the first to organize communities of monks and nuns and to establish monasteries and nunneries. Under cover of the legend of Barlaam and Josaphat, the story of Buddha has found a niche in the row of canonized Catholic saints and has his Saint-day in the calendar of the Greek and Roman churches.

The Buddhist missionaries and preachers also influenced the faith of the Gnostics and Manicheans,* and introduced the idea of reincarnation among them. Many of the early church Fathers, like Origen, admitted that the soul existed before birth and would be born again, that this was not the first or the last time that we had come or would come to this world. The doctrine of pre-existence and reincarnation of souls was accepted by the majority of the Christians until it was suppressed in 538 A.D. by Justinian, who passed this law: "Whoever shall support the mythical presentation of the pre-existence of the soul and the consequently wonderful opinion of its return, let him be Anathema." It was foreign to Judaism until about the eighth century A.D., when under the influence of the Hindu mystics it was adopted by the Karaites and other Jewish sects. The Jewish Encyclopedia says: "Only with the spread of the Cabala did it begin to take root in Judaism, and then it gained

* Professor E. W. Hopkins declares that "Neo-Platonism and Christian Gnosticism owe much to India" in their philosophical beliefs. See p. 25.

believers even among men who were little inclined toward mysticism." And again: "Like Origen and other church Fathers the Cabalists used as their main argument in favor of the doctrine of metempsychosis the justice of God!"*

The Sanskrit grammar of Panini, who, according to Max Müller, was the greatest grammarian that the world has ever seen, has given a key to the science of comparative philology. Many of the English words which we commonly use can be traced back to a Sanskrit origin. For instance: Mother, in Latin *mater*, is in Sanskrit *Mâtar;* father, in Latin *pater*, is in Sanskrit *Pitar;* brother, in Sanskrit *Bhrâtar;* sister, *Swasar;* daughter, *Duhitar;* path, in Sanskrit *Patha;* serpent, *Sarpa;* bond, *Bandha;* etc. The word "punch" has an interesting history. It originally meant "five" in Sanskrit; so the expression, "Give him a punch," means literally "Give him five fingers." We also use the name "punch" for the drink, which implies that it is made up of five ingredients.

In the last lecture, I showed how the fables

* Vol. XII, p. 232.

of Æsop and Pilpay originated in India. Indeed, these stories of animals, with their wonderful Hindu morals, have influenced the young minds of Europe and America for many centuries. I think no child is brought up without studying some of them and learning the morals attached to them. Roman law and Roman jurisprudence also were perhaps not left uninfluenced by the more perfect system of ancient Hindu law.

Now, I will show you the more recent influence of India upon Western civilization. Those who have studied Schopenhauer's philosophy have undoubtedly noticed that he was full of Buddhistic ideas, as well as of the principles of the Vedanta philosophy. He paid a great tribute to the latter by his celebrated saying, "There is no study more beneficial and elevating to mankind than the study of the Upanishads *

* "Fifty Upanishads, under the name of Oupenek'hat, were translated from the Sanskrit into Persian in 1656 at the instance of the Sultan Mohammed Dara Shakoh, and from the Persian into Latin in 1801–2 by Anquetil Duperron."—Philosophy of the Upanishads, Paul Deussen, p. 36.

(Vedanta). It has been the solace of my life, and it will be the solace of my death." And Max Müller declares, "If philosophy is meant to be a preparation for a happy death, or Euthanasia, I know of no better preparation for it than the Vedanta philosophy"; while Schopenhauer's direct disciple, Paul Deussen, writes in his "Philosophy of the Upanishads": "God, the sole author of all good in us, is not, as in the Old Testament, a Being contrasted with and distinct from us, but rather . . . our divine self. This and much more we may learn from the Upanishads: we shall learn the lesson if we are willing to put the finishing touch to the Christian consciousness, and to make it on all sides consistent and complete." In fact, the philosophy of modern Europe has obtained a new life since the introduction of the doctrines of Vedanta into it. Carlyle was influenced by the teachings of Krishna through the English version of the Bhagavad Gita,* first translated by Charles Wilkins during the administration of Warren Hastings, and now well known to you as the

* Published in London in 1785 and in New York in 1867.

"Song Celestial." Many other translations have also been published in Europe and America. Frederick Schlegel, Victor Cousin, Amiel, Paul Deussen, Max Müller, and Emerson were great advocates of the Vedanta philosophy. Emerson was, indeed, the pioneer of Hindu thought in America. He says in his Journal that the study of the Upanishads was a favorite recreation with him. Perhaps you have read his poem on Brahman, which he calls "Brahm"; it begins with this celebrated verse:

> "If the red slayer thinks he slays,
> Or if the slain thinks he is slain,
> They know not well the subtle ways
> I keep, and pass, and turn again."

This is almost a literal translation of a passage in the Bhagavad Gita, which runs thus:

"He who thinketh It to be a slayer and he who thinketh It to be slain,—both of these know not, for It neither killeth nor is killed" (chap. ii, verse 19).

Like Emerson, the Concord sage, Thoreau, was also deeply imbued with the sublime teachings of Vedanta. "The Hindus," he writes, "are more serenely and thoughtfully religious than the Hebrews. They have, perhaps, a purer, more independent, and impersonal knowledge of God. Their religious books describe the first inquisitive and contemplative access to God; the Hebrew Bible, a conscientious return, a grosser and more personal repentance. Repentance is not a free and fair highway to God. A wise man will dispense with repentance. It is shocking and passionate. God prefers that you approach him thoughtfully, not penitent, though you are the chief of sinners. It is only by forgetting yourself that you draw near to Him.

"The calmness and gentleness with which the Hindu philosophers approach and discourse on forbidden themes is admirable.

"What extracts from the Vedas I have read fall on me like the light of a higher and purer luminary, which describes a loftier course through a purer stratum,—free from particulars, simple, universal. It rises on me like the full moon after the stars have come out, wading through some far summer stratum of sky.

"The Vedant teaches how, 'by forsaking religious rites,' the votary may 'obtain purification of mind.'

"One wise sentence is worth the State of Massachusetts many times over.

"The Vedas contain a sensible account of God.

"The religion and philosophy of the Hebrew are those of a wilder and ruder tribe, wanting the civility and intellectual refinement and subtlety of the Hindus.

"I do not prefer one religion or philosophy to another. I have no sympathy with the bigotry and ignorance which makes transient and partial and puerile distinctions between one man's faith and another's, as Christian and heathen. I pray to be delivered from narrowness, partiality, exaggeration, bigotry. To the philosopher, all sects, all nations, are alike. I like Brahma, Hari, or Buddha, the Great Spirit, as well as God."

To-day the whole Western world is permeated with Hindu thoughts and ideals. The educated men and women of Europe and America, who have outgrown the superstitions, doctrines, and dogmas of orthodox Christianity, are finding the right solutions of the problems of life and death, and of the riddles of the universe, as also the greatest comfort and happiness in the universal religion of Vedanta, which is in perfect harmony with the science, logic, and philosophy of modern Europe. To-day the moral influence of Buddhism and the ethics of Vedanta are strongly felt in all European and American communities. You see how many vegetarians are springing up, how many people now prefer a vegetarian diet to animal flesh. I saw the other day in New York a hospital for dogs and cats, but, as I have already told you, such a hospital was built in 260 B.C. by the Buddhist emperor, Asoka. Then, again, the interest in concentration, meditation, breathing exercises, New Thought, etc., which is to be found at present all through Europe and America, is the result of Eastern influence. Mrs. Eddy's early editions of "Science and Health" had quotations from the Bhagavad Gita; and Celia Thaxter, we know, was deeply influenced by the teachings of Krishna, gathered from the same source. The Theosophists have, indeed, disseminated the Hindu teachings most widely all over the world. Even in Mexico I discovered that the teachings of Vedanta were spreading rapidly.

From very ancient times the Hindus as a nation have practised the sublime ethical precept of non-resistance of evil, and the grand moral doctrine of returning good for evil and "love thy neighbor as thyself." "Love thy neighbor as thyself" was taught by Christ, but why? The reason was not given by Him. In the Vedas we find the reason: "Thou shalt love thy neighbor because thou art thy neighbor in spirit. Thou art one with him." "*Tat twam asi*," "That art Thou." Love means expression of oneness. The Hindus have always practised these higher ethical virtues, but as a result India has been invaded again and again by the greedy nations of Europe and Asia. To-day they have been enslaved by the swords of a Christian nation, whose Master proclaimed before the world the doctrine of non-resistance of evil, of returning good for evil, and of loving one's enemies. As nations, the so-called Christian nations of Europe do not follow the path of their Master, do not practise non-resistance of evil, do not love their enemies; on the contrary, they worhip Mammon, and seek worldly success and material prosperity instead of the Kingdom of Heaven. They send missionaries as forerunners of conquest and pioneers for territorial possession. They do not spread peace and goodwill among the people, but fire and guns, as we have seen lately in the British expedition to Tibet. We cannot forget how the poor, innocent Tibetans were mowed down by Maxim guns. We cannot forget how the Portuguese and Dutch Christians held in one hand the Bible and in the other a gun, and demolished the Hindu temples in India. We cannot forget how the Christian missionaries, under the name of religion, destroyed the monuments of Buddhism in Japan until they were driven out by the Japanese Government in 1614 A.D. The Hindu and Buddhist missionaries, on the contrary, have always carried, instead of fire and sword, the gospel of peace and goodwill, and have civilized the nations.

Think what Buddhism has done for China and Japan, for Tibet and Burmah! The whole civilization of Japan is indebted to Buddhism for its art, as for most other things. Buddhism was introduced into Japan in the sixth century after Christ, and since that time has lived there in absolute peace and harmony with Shintoism and Confucianism. Buddhism was introduced into China in 65 A.D., and it has existed among the Chinese for nearly two thousand years without destroying anything of Taoism and Confucianism, at the same time broadening the religious ideals of the nation, humanizing and civilizing them. Lafcadio Hearn, in his book on Japan, shows how much Buddhism has done for Japan; and those who have read "The Soul of a People," by H. Fielding Hall, cannot help admiring the humane, loving, and spiritual qualities of the Buddhist people. Religious toleration has always been practised by the Hindus and Buddhists. When the Parsees were driven out of Persia by the Mohometans, they took refuge in India, where they are now flourishing and living unmolested. Under the influence of this religious toleration of the Hindus, Western nations, especially the English, are beginning to learn and practise it. The Hindus and Buddhists have never robbed their neighbors to enrich themselves, but they have given to the world the highest moral and spiritual truths, not in mere theories, but by setting their noble examples. The Hindus and Buddhists have always been the true spiritual teachers of the world; they know how to preach and how to live religion. By a strange irony of fate, to-day they are called barbarous and uncivilized heathens by the aggressive pioneers of European conquest.*

Practical morality and spirituality have always been considered by the Hindus as greater than mere intellectual culture. In India, religion has been the source of philosophy, science, art, music, and everything. From religion the Hindus have gained their education and culture, therefore religion is a vital thing with them. It is the primary thing, while intellectual cul-

* "Unhappy Asia! Do you call it unhappy Asia? this land of divine needs and divine thought! Its slumber is more vital than the waking life of the rest of the globe, as the dream of genius is more precious than the vigils of ordinary men. Unhappy Asia, do you call it? It is the unhappiness of Europe over which I mourn." Benjamin Disraeli (Lord Beaconsfield).

ture is secondary. The Hindus cultivate the feelings of the heart and do not care much for external reforms. It is for this reason that their civilization is based upon the highest moral and spiritual standards. Hindu civilization is founded, not upon the commercial and industrial interests of the people, but upon the eternal moral and spiritual laws which govern our lives. It is not like the European civilization of to-day, which inspires a nation mainly to protect its self-interest at the expense of other nations, and to gain material and commercial prosperity by depriving others of their rights, by robbing the weaker nations who are kind, innocent, and humane.

According to the Hindu idea, that man is civilized who is versed in the Scriptures; who is learned and wise in the various branches of knowledge; who is truthful, unselfish, and who obeys the moral laws; who helps the poor and distressed; who returns good for evil; and who conquers hatred by love, avarice by generosity. These are the high moral virtues which should adorn the character of a thoroughly civilized man. A civilized man must always cultivate these virtues, and control the brute impulses and animal propensities with which he is born. By these virtues the civilized man is distinguished from a barbarous savage, as also from lower animals. A civilized man or woman must have polished manners, not simply as an external form, as we see in Europe to-day, but they must proceed from the feelings of the heart. European civilization,* on the contrary, has left moral and spiritual standards in the background, and made material prosperity and intellectual culture the chief factors of civilization. The old brutal law of "might is right" is still in its ascendancy in the civilization of the West. The West looks mainly to externals, but India looks chiefly to the internal. With the former, worldly prosperity is the goal, and intellectual preëmi-

* "Asia revivified would act upon Europe. The European comfort, which they call civilization, is, after all, confined to a very small space,—the Island of Great Britain, France, and the course of a single river, the Rhine. The greater part of Europe is as dead as Asia, without the consolation of climate and the influence of immortal traditions."—Benjamin Disraeli (Lord Beaconsfield).

nence is its watchword. With the latter, the attainment of spiritual perfection is the highest aim of civilization, and the cultivation of moral virtues is a necessary step or auxiliary. In Europe, religion has always retarded the progress of true civilization and freedom of thought by the Inquisition, and by continuous persecution on the part of priests and clergy. Think of the fate of Galileo, Giardino Bruno, and a host of other eminent thinkers of the Middle Ages! Consequently religion has been put aside from practical daily life. But freedom of thought must be the constant companion of true civilization. Social and political freedom are also the outcome of the most advanced kind of civilization. Freedom is the goal for every man, but that freedom must be based upon moral and spiritual laws.

Through the influence of the dominant or rather militant civilization of Europe, India has lost her social and political freedom. She has become a slave. She cannot talk freely; she cannot discuss the unjust policy and oppressive methods of the so-called civilized government which rules over her. European civilization has given to India the standard of commercialism, and has set an example of extreme selfishness, and this has been undermining the moral and spiritual standards of the Hindus. The ideal of simplicity and of humanitarianism is every day sacrificed upon the altar of commercialism and greed for material possession. Those who try to live in India a Christ-like life of purity and righteousness are robbed and dispossessed of their property by the selfish pioneers of the aggressive civilization of England. Under the influence of British rule, the culture of the feelings of the heart among the younger generation has become almost an impossibility. The moral and spiritual standards of the Hindus are giving place to hypocrisy and intellectual culture for material gain. The vices of Christian civilization, with slaughter-houses and saloons, with the liquor trade and the opium trade as Government monopolies for revenue, have been spreading all over India under the civilizing power of English rule.

The influence of Western civilization is destroying the social structure of the Hindus, and is breaking the harmony of the household life which has existed from time immemorial. But it has done some good. It has loosened the rigidity of caste rules and caste distinctions, and has removed the degenerating evil effects of priestcraft. India was groaning under priestcraft, but to-day its evil effects have been removed by English education. English education, on the other hand, has disturbed the minds of the people; has shaken their faith in their religion; has made its students advocates of atheism, agnosticism, and utilitarianism, which are the banes of scientific education. The great mass of Hindu students who come out of the universities every year do not believe in God or the human soul, do not care for anything but worldly success, social position, fame, and glory. Their first object in life is to earn their bread and butter by some honest profession. The heartless and demoralizing influence of business competition, which never existed under caste rules in India, is suppressing the moral and spiritual development of the people. The gladiatorial policy of

European civilization is now in full force. The educated Hindus of to-day do not know which step to take in the path of their worldly career. They run for help toward the governing power, as a child would run to its father for protection in time of distress, but their hearts are filled with despair when they meet the frowning eyes of task-masters under the garb of Western culture and civilization. A civilized Englishman in India kicks his native servant to death, and is fined perhaps five dollars by the Government. A civilized Englishman on a tea plantation in Assam will carry on a coolie trade, which is almost as bad as the old slave-trade, and is seldom punished by the Government. Such are the examples which the Hindus are witnessing every day in India.

Western civilization under British rule has opened the eyes of the masses, has made them realize that a foreign government is no better than a curse of God upon a nation; and a nation which tyrannizes over another nation for its own gain is not entitled to be called civilized, according to the Hindu standard of civilization.

But I must say that India has derived certain benefits from English rule. After one hundred and fifty years of oppression and tyranny, it has made the Hindus stand on their own feet, and has brought out their national and patriotic feelings, in which they were lacking for nearly a century. It has brought India in close touch with European and American culture, and has driven away many superstitious ideas from the minds of the Hindus. The Hindus are now taking lessons in commercialism from the civilized masters of Europe, and are studying their ways and manners, so that in future they will be able to become their worthy disciples. Japan has shown to the world what ready disciples of Western civilization her people have become in less than half a century. Now it will be the turn for poor and downtrodden India. We may not see it, but future generations will enjoy that freedom which is the goal of all nations.

Another good thing has come from the influence of Western civilization, and that is the blessing of scientific education for the masses. It has opened a new field, and has brought a tremendous power of knowledge with it. India is beginning to wake up from her sleep in the darkness which prevailed during the night of the Mahometan rule of six hundred years, and her children are now receiving the light of science and the blessings of knowledge which have come from her contact with England. India will always remain gratefully indebted to the West, especially to England, for this blessing, and will always thank the Lord that He has given to her people so glorious an opportunity to accomplish her future greatness and political regeneration. India needs the spirit of Western civilization, while the West needs yet to learn from the Hindus the lesson of religious toleration, as also that practical method by which it will establish its civilization upon the principles of higher ethics and true spirituality taught by the universal religion of Vedanta, which is the crest jewel of the civilization of India.

WOMAN'S PLACE IN HINDU RELIGION.

VII.

WOMAN'S PLACE IN HINDU RELIGION.

WELL has it been said by Louis Jaccoliot, the celebrated French author of the "Bible in India," that: "India of the Vedas entertained a respect for women amounting to worship; a fact which we seem little to suspect in Europe when we accuse the extreme East of having denied the dignity of woman, and of having only made of her an instrument of pleasure and of passive obedience." He also said: "What! Here is a civilization, which you cannot deny to be older than your own, which places the woman on a level with the man and gives her an equal place in the family and in society."

Long before the civil laws of the Romans, which gave the foundation for the legislation of Europe and of America, were codified by Justinian, the Hindu laws of Manu were closely observed and strictly followed by the members of Hindu society in general. Many of the Oriental scholars, having compared the digest of Justinian and the Mosaic laws of the Old Testament with the Hindu laws, have arrived at the conclusion that the code of Manu was related to them as a father is to his child. Yet the Hindu law-givers only repeated and codified the ethical principles which were inculcated in the Vedas. Following the teachings of the Vedas, the Hindu legislator gave equal rights to men and women by saying: "Before the creation of this phenomenal universe, the first-born Lord of all creatures divided his own self into two halves, so that one half should be male and the other half female." This illustration has established in the minds of the Hindus the fundamental equality of man and woman. Just as the equal halves of a fruit possess the same nature, the same attributes, and the same properties in equal proportion, so man and woman, being the equal halves of the same substance, possess equal rights, equal privileges, and equal powers. This idea of the equality of man and woman was the corner-stone of that huge structure of religion and ethics among the Hindus which has stood for so many ages the ravages of time and change, defying the onslaughts of the short-sighted critics of the world. Therefore, in India, whatever is claimed for the man may also be claimed for the woman; there should be no partiality shown for either man or woman, according to the ethical, moral, and religious standards of the Hindus.

The same idea of equality was most forcibly expressed in the Rig Veda (Book 5, hymn 61, verse 8). The commentator explains this passage thus: "The wife and husband, being the equal halves of one substance, are equal in every respect; therefore both should join and take equal parts in all work, religious and secular." No other Scriptures of the world have ever given to the woman such equality with the man as the Vedas of the Hindus. The Old Testament, the Koran, and the Zend-Avesta have made woman the scapegoat for all the crimes committed by man. The Old Testament, in describing the creation of woman and the fall of man, has established the idea that woman was created for man's pleasure; consequently her duty was to obey him implicitly. It makes her an instrument in the hands of Satan for the temptation and fall of the holy man with whom she was enjoying the felicity of paradise. Adam's first thought on that occasion was to shift the burden of guilt on to the shoulders of the woman. St. Paul, in the New Testament, shows that, through Adam's fall, woman was the means of bringing sin, suffering, and death into the wor'd. Popular Christianity has been trying lately to take away this idea, but, in spite of all the efforts of the preachers, it still lurks behind the eulogies that have been piled upon the conception of womanhood in Christian lands. How is it possible, for one who believes the accounts given in Genesis to be literally true, to reject the idea there set forth that woman was the cause of the temptation and fall of man, thereby bringing sin and suffering and death into the world? For one who accepts the Biblical account, there is no other alternative left.

In India, such ideas never arose in the minds

of the Vedic seers, nor have kindred notions found expression in the writings of the law-givers of later days. The Hindu legislators realized that both sexes were equal, and said before the world that women had equal rights with men for freedom, for the acquirement of knowledge, education, and spirituality. It is for this reason that we find in the Rig Veda the names of so many inspired women who attained to the realization of the highest spiritual truths. These inspired women are recognized by all classes as the Seers of Truth, as spiritual instructors, divine speakers and revealers, equally with the inspired men of Vedic hymns. Those who believe that the Hindu religion debars women from studying the Vedas, or from acquiring religious ideas ought to correct these erroneous notions by opening their eyes to the facts, which are indelibly written on the pages of the religious history of India. The one hundred and twenty-sixth hymn of the first book of the Rig Veda was revealed by a Hindu woman whose name was Romashâ; the one hundred and seventy-ninth hymn of the same book was by Lopâmudrâ, another inspired

Hindu woman. I can cite at least a dozen names of women revealers of the Vedic wisdom, such as Visvavârâ, Shashvati, Gârgi, Maitreyi, Apâlâ, Ghoshâ, and Aditî, who instructed Indra, one of the Devas, in the higher knowledge of Brahman, the Universal Spirit. All of these are the names of inspired women revealers of the spiritual wisdom. Every one of them lived the ideal life of spirituality, being untouched by the things of the world. They are called in Sanskrit Brahmavâdinîs, the speakers and revealers of Brahman. They were devout performers of the religious rites, singers of holy hymns, and often discussed with great philosophers the most subtle problems of life and death, the nature of the soul and of God, and their inter-relation, and sometimes, in the course of these discussions, they defeated the most advanced thinkers among their opponents.

Those who have read the Upanishads, the philosophical portions of the Vedas, know that Gârgi and Maitreyi, the two great women Seers of Truth, discoursed on philosophical topics with Yâjnavalka, who was one of the best authorities in the Vedic lore. There are many instances of women acting as arbitrators on such occasions. When Sankarâchârya, the great commentator of the Vedanta, was discussing this philosophy with another philosopher, a Hindu lady, well versed in all the Scriptures, was requested to act as umpire.

If, in the face of such facts, the Christian missionaries say that the Hindu religion prevents women from studying the Vedas, or denies them a place in religion, we can only console ourselves by thinking that the eyes of our missionary brothers and sisters are not open to truths which exist outside the boundary-line of their own particular creed and religion. It is the especial injunction of the Vedas that no married man shall perform any religious rite, ceremony, or sacrifice without being joined in it by his wife; should he do so, his work will be incomplete and half finished, and he will not get the full results, because the wife is considered to be a partaker and partner in the spiritual life of her husband: she is called, in Sanskrit, *Sahadharminî*, "spiritual helpmate." This idea is very old, as old as the Hindu nation. It is true that there were certain prohibitions for some women against certain studies and ceremonies, which were prescribed for those only who were in a different stage of spiritual development, just as a certain class of men were proscribed from the studies of some portions of the Vedas, or from performing certain ceremonies simply because they were not ready for them.

Coming down from the Vedic period to the time when the Purânas and Epics were written, we find that the same idea of equality between men and women was kept alive, and that the same laws were observed as during the time of the Vedas. Those who have read the Râmâyana will remember how exemplary was the character of Sitâ, the heroine. She was the embodiment of purity, chastity, and kindness, the personification of spirituality. She still stands as the perfect type of ideal womanhood in the hearts of the Hindu women of all castes and creeds. In the whole religious history of the world a second Sitâ will not be found. Her life was unique. She is worshipped as an Incarnation of God, as Christ is worshipped among the Christians. India is the only country where prevails a belief that God incarnates in the form of a woman as well as in that of a man.

In the Mahâbhârata we read the account of Sulabhâ, the great woman Yogi, who came to the court of King Janaka and showed wonderful powers and wisdom, which she had acquired through the practice of Yoga. This shows that women were allowed to practise Yoga; even to-day there are many living *Yoginîs* in India who are highly advanced in spirituality. Many of these *Yoginîs* become spiritual teachers of men. Sri Râmakrishna, the greatest Saint of the nineteenth century, was taught spiritual truths by a *Yoginî*.*

As in religion the Hindu woman of ancient times enjoyed equal rights and privileges with men, so in secular matters she had equal share and equal power with them. From the Vedic age women in India have had the same right to possess property as men; they could go to the

* See "Life and Sayings of Râmakrishna," by Prof. F. Max Müller, published by Scribner and Sons, New York.

courts of justice, plead their own cases, and ask for the protection of the law.

Those who have read the famous Hindu drama, called Sakuntalâ, know that Sakuntalâ pleaded her own case and claimed her rights in the court of King Dushyanta. Similar instances are mentioned in the one hundred and eighth hymn of the tenth book of the Rig Veda. As early as 2000 B.C. Hindu women were allowed to go to the battle-fields to fight against enemies. Saramâ, one of the most powerful women of her day, was sent by her husband in search of robbers. She discovered their hiding-place and afterwards destroyed them.

In the fifth book of the Rig Veda we read that King Namuchi sent his wife to fight against his enemies. She fought and eventually conquered them. There have been many instances of women holding high political powers, governing states, making laws, and administering justice to all. Throughout the history of India are to be found the names of many women who have governed their own territories. Some women of later dates resisted foreign invaders.* The history of India records the wonderful generalship of the *Râni* of Jhânsi, who held a portion of the British army in check during the famous mutiny of 1857–58. She headed her troops against the British, dressed like a cavalry officer, and after a hard fight she fell in battle and died, in June, 1858. Sir Hugh Rose declared that the best man on the enemy's side was the *Râni* of Jhânsi, not knowing that the *Râni* was not a man, but the Queen herself.

Not long ago a Hindu lady, Aus Kour by name, was elevated by the Hindus, with the help of the British Government, to the disputed throne of the disorganized and revolted State of Patiâlâ, in the northwest of India. She has been described by English historians as the most competent person to govern that state. In less than a year she brought peace and security into all parts of her dominions.

Ahalyâ Bai, the Queen of Mâlwâ, governed

* The heroic queen Chând Bibi, who defended the fort of Ahmednagar against the attacks of the Mogul emperor Akbar, may be called the Joan of Arc of India.

her kingdom with great success for twenty years, devoting herself to the rights and welfare of her people and the happiness of her subjects; she was so great and popular that both the Mahometans and the Hindus united in prayers for her long life; so little did she care for name and fame that, when a book was written in her honor, she ordered it to be destroyed, and took no notice of the author.

America boasts of her civilization and the freedom of her women, but we know how little power and how few privileges have been given to women. The cause of this is deeply rooted in the Biblical conception of womanhood. It is claimed that Christianity has elevated the condition of women; but, on the contrary, history tells us that it is Christianity that has stood for centuries in the way of the religious, social, and political freedom of women. Think of the women's suffrage societies, and how hard they are struggling to win recognition of the rights of their sex.* Roman law and Roman juris-

* The following extract from a letter sent by Mrs. Elizabeth Cady Stanton to Bishop Potter, of New York,

prudence gave woman a place far more elevated than that given to her by Christianity. The Christians learned to honor women from the pagans. The Teutonic tribes believed, like the Hindus, in the perfect equality of both sexes in all domestic and social relations, and held that a queen was as good as a king. Even to-day the Christian nations fail to see this equality between man and woman.

---

on 15th January, 1901, will give an idea of the situation:

"Ever and anon public thought is aroused by a terrible tragedy, like the one enacted in Paterson, or by some unusually open manifestation of vice in the streets of our cities. Though an aroused public sentiment can repress the evils for a time in one locality, they reappear at once, with renewed energy, in many others. Occasionally, church officials make their protests, but no one seems to understand the hidden cause of all these outrages.

"The authorities of the Episcopal Church are just now aroused to action. The first step to be taken is to teach woman a higher respect for herself, and the rising generation a more profound reverence.

"The Church and the Bible make woman the football for the jibes and jeers of the multitude.

"When, in their marriage service, it is the duty of woman to obey, and be given away by some man, she is made the inferior and subject of man.

"All our efforts to suppress the social evil are hopeless until woman is recognized, in the canon law and all

The Hindu law allows the women a much greater share in the management of property than most of the statutes of the Christian nations. In family affairs, religious or secular, especially in business or trade, a husband in India cannot take any step without consulting the female members of the family.

It is often said that Hindu women are treated like slaves by their husbands, but it is not a fact. On the contrary, the Hindu women get better treatment than the majority of the wives

---

church discipline, as equal in goodness to bishops. archbishops, and the Pope himself.

"The sentiments of men in high places are responsible for the outrages on woman in the haunts of vice and on the highway. If the same respect the masses are educated to feel for cathedrals, altars, symbols, and sacraments were extended to the mothers of the race, as it should be, all these problems would be speedily settled.

"When our good men in State and Church try to suppress the terrible outrages on woman, while they deal with the evil on the surface, they should begin the lasting work of securing to her equal honor, dignity, and respect by sharing with her all the liberties they themselves enjoy.

"The lesson of inferiority is taught everywhere, and in these terrible tragedies of life we have the result of the universal degradation of woman."

of Englishmen or of Americans endowed with the spirit of an English husband. Sir Monier Monier Williams says: "Indian wives often possess greater influence than the wives of Europeans." The number of wife-beaters is considerably smaller in India than in Europe or America. He is not a true Hindu who does not regard a woman's body as sacred as the temple of God. He is an outcast who touches a woman's body with irreverence, hatred, or anger. "A woman's body," says Manu the law-giver, "must not be struck hard, even with a flower, because it is sacred." It is for this reason that the Hindus do not allow capital punishment for women. The treatment of woman, according to Hindu religion, will be better understood from some of the quotations from the laws of Manu and other law-givers. Manu says:

1. "The mouth of a woman is always pure." V, 130.

2. "Women must be honored and adorned by their fathers, husbands, brothers, and brothers-in-law, who desire their own welfare." III, 55.

3. "Where women are honored, there the Devas

(gods) are pleased; but where they are dishonored, no sacred rite yields rewards." III, 56.

4. "Where female relations live in grief, the family soon wholly perishes; but that family where they are not unhappy ever prospers." III, 57.

5. "In like manner, care must be taken of barren women, of those who have no sons, of those whose family is extinct, of wives and widows faithful to their lords, and of women afflicted with diseases." VIII, 28.

6. "A righteous king must punish like thieves those relatives who appropriate the property of such females during their lifetime." VIII, 29.

7. "In order to protect women and Brâhmins, he who kills in the cause of right commits no sin." VIII, 349.

8. "One's daughter is the highest object of tenderness; hence, if one is offended by her, one must bear it without resentment." IV, 185. (Compare this with the statements of the missionaries that the Hindu religion sanctions the killing of girls.)

9. "A maternal aunt, the wife of a maternal

uncle, a mother-in-law, and a paternal aunt, must be honored like the wife of one's spiritual teacher; they are equal to the wife of one's spiritual teacher." II, 131.

(In India, the wife of a spiritual teacher is regarded as a living goddess.)

10. "Towards the sister of one's father and of one's mother and towards one's elder sister, one must behave as towards one's mother; but the mother is more venerable than they." II, 133.

11. "But the teacher is ten times more venerable than the sub-teacher, the father a hundred times more than the teacher, but the mother a thousand times more than the father." II, 145.

12. "A chaste wife, who after the death of her husband constantly remains chaste, reaches heaven, though she have no son, just like those chaste men." V, 160. (Compare this with the statements of the missionaries that Hindu widows are cursed by their religion.)

13. "In that family where the husband is pleased with his wife and the wife with her husband, happiness will assuredly be lasting." III, 60.

14. "Offspring, the due performance of religious rites, faithful service, highest conjugal happiness, and heavenly bliss for the ancestors and one's self, depend upon the wife alone." IX, 28.

15. "Let mutual fidelity continue till death; this may be considered as a summary of the highest law for husband and wife." IX, 101.

From other Hindu laws:

"Woman possesses an unequalled means of purification: they never become (entirely) foul."

"Women are pure in all limbs."

1. "Man is strength, woman is beauty; he is the reason that governs and she is the wisdom that moderates."

2. "He who despises woman despises his mother."

3. "He who is cursed by a woman is cursed by God."

4. "The tears of a woman call down the fire of heaven on those who make them flow."

5. "Evil to him who laughs at a woman's sufferings; God shall laugh at his prayers."

6. "The songs of women are sweet in the ears

of the Lord; men should not, if they wish to be heard, sing the praises of God without women."

7. "There is no crime more odious than to persecute women, and to take advantage of their weakness to despoil them of their patrimony."

8. "The woman watches over the house, and the protecting divinities (Devas) of the domestic hearth are happy in her presence. The labors of the field should never be assigned to her."

9. "When relatives, by some subterfuge, take possession of the property of a woman, her carriages or her jewels, such evil-doers shall descend into the infernal regions."

10. "The virtuous woman should have but one husband, as the right-minded man should have but one wife."

Here is the definition of a wife given in the Mahâbhârata:—

> A wife is half the man, his truest friend;
> A loving wife is a perpetual spring
> Of virtue, pleasure, wealth; a faithful wife
> Is his best aid in seeking heavenly bliss;
> A sweetly-speaking wife is a companion
> In solitude, a father in advice,
> A mother in all seasons of distress,
> A rest in passing through life's wilderness."

The Christian missionaries say that these laws are most horrible! Yet to-day in some parts of Europe women are yoked together with horses and cattle in the field, and obliged to do the roughest labor!

The unmarried daughter, not the son, inherits the mother's estate. This is the Hindu law. The special property of the wife which she gets as dowry cannot be used by the husband. A wife in India is not responsible for the debts of her husband or son. The mother in India owns her children as much as the father does.

Mrs. F. A. Steele, who has written several novels on Indian life, and who resided in India for twenty-five years, writes of Indian women: "In regard to the general position of women in India, I think it is rather better than our own. Women in India can hold property, and a widow always gets a fixed portion of her husband's estate."

Some American ladies who lived in India, not as missionaries but as impartial observers, have corroborated these statements. It is generally said that the Hindu law makes no provision for the Hindu widows. Let us see what an English historian says:

"In the absence of direct male heirs, widows succeed to a life-interest in real and absolute interest in personal property. The daughters inherit absolutely. Where there are sons, mothers and daughters are entitled to shares, and wives hold peculiar property from a variety of sources over which a husband has no control during their lives, and which descends to their own heirs, with a preference to females." *

Much has been said against the marriage customs of the Hindus. I have heard a great deal of objection to them, in this country especially. It is true that marriage by courtship is not considered by the Hindus to be the highest and best system; they say this method generally proceeds from selfish desires, or the mere gratification of passion. Marriage, according to the Hindu ideas, must be based on the ideal of the spiritual union of the souls, and not on the lower desires for sense pleasures. It must be a sacred bond. The Hindus were the first to

* Mill's History of India, Vol. I, p. 248.

recognize marriage as an indissoluble holy bond between two souls. Even death does not dissolve it; and this idea prevails in the hearts of many Hindu wives, who do not care to remarry after the death of their husbands, but prefer to devote their lives to fulfilling spiritual duties.

Mrs. Steele says: "I have seen many a virgin widow who gloried in her fate." Marriage is not considered to be the only aim of life. There are nobler and higher purposes, and they must be accomplished before death comes. The whole spirit of the marriage laws in India is in favor of the legal union between one man and one woman, but they allow a little latitude for the preservation of the race. It is said that a man may marry a second wife for progeny alone, with the consent of his first wife, in case she should be barren.

The aim of Hindu law-givers was to build a society where the moral and spiritual evolution of the individual should be free from legal interference. Therefore they divided society into classes, and set forth laws for each class; the marriage laws in India have been many-sided in order to suit the different tendencies which prevailed among different classes. Hindu law-givers understood that one law would not do for all people. The higher the class in society, the more restricted are their laws; for instance, the same law-giver, who allows the marriage of widows amongst the lower classes, sets forth arguments against its practice among women of a higher class. Nearly all Hindu widows of the lower classes can remarry after the death of their husbands; but it depends upon the choice both of the husband and the wife. The Hindu law provides for the remarriage of widows * and of divorced women in the same way as for the remarriage of widowers and divorced men. According to the law, a wife may abandon her husband (if she choose) if he be criminal, insane,

* "That the remarriage of widows in Vedic times was a national custom can be easily established by a variety of proofs and arguments. The very fact of the Sanskrit language having from ancient times such words as *didhishu*, 'a man that has married a widow,' *parapurva*, 'a woman that has taken a second husband,' *paunarbhava*, 'a son of a woman by her second husband,' are enough to establish it."—"Indo-Arians," by Rajendra Lala Mitra, Vol. II, p. 155.

impotent, outcast, or afflicted with leprosy, also because of his long absence in foreign lands, and can take another husband. The Roman law gives no other causes of divorce than these. Similarly, a husband may abandon his wife if she be drunken or adulterous, afflicted with leprosy, or cruel towards husband and children, and can remarry. But the Hindu law does not allow a divorce simply for incompatibility of temper, nor because of the simple desire in either party to marry another.

It is said that the greatest curse is the child-marriage in India, and that it is sanctioned by religion; but this is not true. Religion distinctly forbids it, and in many parts of India so-called child-marriage is nothing but a betrothal. The betrothal ceremony takes place some years before the real marriage ceremony; sufficient cause may prolong the period of betrothal for even three or four years. In Northern India the real marriage does not take place until the parties are of proper age; it is attended with music, feasting, and the presentation of gifts. A betrothed wife stays in her father's house until the time of her real marriage. In Southern India, customs are not the same; many abuses have crept in, and child-wives are often given to their husbands at too tender an age. The Hindu law does not prevent the remarriage of the betrothed wife after the death of her betrothed husband, but it says that under such circumstances the parents of the betrothed wife commit a sin as of giving false witness before the court of justice.

According to the Hindu law, it is better for a girl of a high caste to remain unmarried for life than to marry one who is not of noble birth or from a family of the same caste, or one who is unqualified and illiterate.

Eight different kinds of marriages are described and discussed by Hindu legislators,* among which marriage with the consent of the parents of both parties, and not a sentimental love contract, is considered to be the highest. In ancient times, when the country was governed by Hindu kings, the *Svayambara* system of marriage was very common. It was the system of free choice

* Manu, III, 21—33.

of a husband by the maiden. Those who have read "The Light of Asia," by Sir Edwin Arnold, will remember how Buddha was married. But when the Hindus lost their political freedom they would have been unable to prevent the intermixture of races had such liberty been continued; so they abandoned that system of marriage and adopted that of betrothing their sons and daughters in their youth. The betrothal, however, is not practised in all parts of the country.

Christian missionaries have brought false charges against the moral character of Hindu women; and some of our own countrywomen, having enlisted their names as Christian converts, have, I regret to say, joined these missionary detractors in bringing false charges against Hindu women. If you wish to know the true condition of the women in India, you will have to reject ninety-nine per cent of the statements which you hear from the missionaries, or from Christian converts who come from India. There are immoral women in India, as there are in every other country, but it is more than wicked to make such sweeping statements as that there is no morality among Hindu women. The Panditâ Ramâbai said: "I would not trust one of my girls in any Indian home. The immorality in that country is horrible!" *

Self-burning of widows was not sanctioned by the Vedic religion, but was due to other causes. Some say that, when the Mahometans conquered India, they treated the widows of the soldiers so brutally that the women preferred death, and voluntarily sought it. It is often said that the "Christian government" has suppressed *Suttee;* but the truth is, that the initiative in this direction was taken by that noble Hindu, Râjah Râm Mohan Roy, who was, however, obliged to secure the aid of the British Government in enforcing his ideas, because India was a subject nation. The educated classes among the Hindus had strongly protested against the priests † who supported this inhuman custom (which prevailed only in certain parts of India), and efforts had been made to suppress the evil by force; but, as it could not be done without

---

* *Fitchburg Sentinel*, 18 April, 1898.

† Brâhminism and Hinduism, p. 482.

official help, appeal was made to the Viceroy, Lord Bentinck, and a law against *Suttee* was passed. Thus the evil was practically suppressed by the Hindus themselves, aided by the British Government.

Sir Monier Monier Williams says: "Perhaps the most important point to which he (Râjah Râm Mohan Roy) awakened attention was the absence of all Vedic sanction for the self-immolation of widows (Suttee, in Sanskrit Sati). It was principally his vehement denunciation of this practice, and the agitation against it set on foot by him, which ultimately led to the abolition of Sati throughout British India in 1829." *

The exclusion of women from the society of men, which we find in some parts of India, is not due to their religion, but to other causes. Although this custom existed among the aristo-

* Some of the Brâhmin priests perverted the meaning of the Vedic text which describes the funeral ceremony of the ancient Hindus. The true meaning of that verse is: "Rise up, woman, thou art lying by one whose life is gone; come, come to the world of the living, away from thy husband, and become the wife of him who grasps thy hand and is willing to marry thee."—Rig Veda, Bk. 10, Hymn 18, verse 8.

cratic classes of the Hindu community, still it came into practice largely for self-defence against Mahometan brutality. The *Purda* system, that is, the custom of not allowing women to appear in public without a veil, was not of Hindu origin, but was introduced into India by the Mahometans. There are many parts of India where the *Purda* system does not exist at all, where men mix freely with women, travel in the same vehicle, and appear in public with the women unveiled. Sir Monier Monier Williams writes: "Moreover, it must be noted that the seclusion and ignorance of women, which were once mainly due to the fear of the Mahometan conquerors, do not exist in the same degree in provinces unaffected by those conquerors."

Every one has heard the old missionary tale of the Hindu mothers throwing their babies to the crocodiles in the Ganges. Touching pictures of a black mother with a white baby in her arms, calmly awaiting the advent of a large crocodile, have adorned many Sunday-school books. Perhaps this story arose from the fact that in certain places poor Hindu mothers place the dead bodies of their little ones by the river-side, because they cannot afford the expense of cremating them.

The zeal of the pious missionaries for Christianizing India was the cause of the story of the car of Jaggannath. Sir Monier Monier Williams says: "It is usual for missionaries to speak with horror of the self-immolation alleged to take place under the car of Jaggannath. But, if deaths occur, they must be accidental, as self-destruction is wholly opposed both to the letter and spirit of their religion." *

As regards female infanticide, Panditâ Ramâbai herself wrote:

"Female infanticide, *though not sanctioned by religion and never looked upon as right* by conscientious people, has nevertheless, in those parts of India mentioned been silently passed over unpunished by society in general." †

The Panditâ does not perhaps know that numbers of dead bodies of illegitimate babies are picked up every year in the streets and

* Brâhmanism and Hinduism, p. 118.

† High-caste Hindu Women, p. 26.

vacant lots of New York and other large American cities. What does American society do about such criminals? Is it not equally reasonable to charge these evils to the Christian religion as to lay all the sins of India at the door of the Hindu religion?

High-caste Hindu women generally learn to read and write in their own vernacular, but they do not pass public examinations. Hindu religion does not prevent any woman from receiving education; on the contrary, it says that it is the duty of the parents, brothers, and husbands to educate their daughters, sisters, and wives. So, if there be ignorance among Hindu women, it is not the fault of their religion, but rather of their poverty.

Malabar boasts of seven great poets, and four of them were women. The moral sentiments uttered by one of them (Avyar) are taught in the schools as the golden rules of life. The writings of Lilâvati, a great woman mathematician, still form the text-book in native schools of the Hindus.

It is often said by the Christian missionaries

that Hindu religion teaches that women have no souls, and that they are not entitled to salvation. On the contrary, all the sacred books of the Hindus testify against such outrageous falsities. Those who have read the Bhagavad Gita, or the Upanishads, know that, according to Hindu religion the soul is sexless, and that all men and women will sooner or later reach the highest goal of religion. It was in India that women were first allowed to be spiritual teachers and to enter into the monastic life. Those who have read the life of Buddha know that his wife became the leader of the Buddhist nuns. There are to-day hundreds of Hindu *Sannyâsinis* (nuns) who are recognized as spiritual teachers by the Hindus. The wife of Sri Râmakrishna, the great Hindu Saint of the nineteenth century, has become a living example of the great honor and reverence that are paid by Hindus to a woman of pure, spotless, spiritual life.

Lastly, the position of women in Hindu religion can be understood better by that unique idea of the Motherhood of God, which is nowhere so strongly expressed and recognized as in India.

The mother is so highly honored in India that the Hindus are not satisfied until they see divinity in the form of earthly mother. They say that one mother is greater than a thousand fathers, therefore the Hindus prefer to call the Supreme Being the Mother of the Universe. The Divine Mother is greater than the "Creator" of other religions. She is the *Producer* of the Creator, or the First-born Lord of all creatures. There is no other country in the world where every living mother is venerated as an incarnation of the Divine Mother, where every village has a guardian mother who protects all as her own children.

Listen to the prayer that rises every day to the Almighty Mother of the universe from the hearts of Hindu worshippers:

"O Mother Divine, Thou art beyond the reach of our praises; Thou pervadest every particle of the universe; all knowledge proceeds from Thee, O Infinite Source of wisdom! Thou dwellest in every feminine form, and all women are Thy living representatives upon earth."